GW01315882

Sneeze and Be Slain
and Other Incredible Stories

Sneeze and Be Slain

and Other Incredible Stories

NORMAN HUNTER

With illustrations by
BABETTE COLE

THE BODLEY HEAD
LONDON   SYDNEY
TORONTO

To my five fine grandsons, Christopher,
Philip, David, Mark and Craig, with love

ACKNOWLEDGEMENTS

'King Jan the First'
first appeared in *Puffin Post*,
December 1978

British Library Cataloguing
in Publication Data
Hunter, Norman
Sneeze and be slain
and other incredible stories.
I. Title
823'.9'1J   PZ7.H9178
ISBN 0-370-30313-X

Text © Norman Hunter 1980
Illustrations © Babette Cole 1980
Printed in Great Britain for
The Bodley Head Ltd
9 Bow Street, London WC2E 7AL
by Redwood Burn Ltd
Trowbridge & Esher
Set in Monotype Baskerville
by Gloucester Typesetting Ltd
First published 1980

CONTENTS

I

Sneeze and Be Slain

The Royal Palace of Incrediblania felt like the inside of an oven ready for cooking a heavy banquet. It was as if twenty-five summers had decided to take place all at once. You could have fried an egg on the floors, only it wouldn't have been hygienic. There were blazing fires in all the rooms and two or three in some. There were hot-water bottles on the chairs as well as in the beds, and steam was coming out of everybody's ears.

'Phew!' moaned the King, mopping his forehead with a handful of tissues because the Queen wouldn't let him use too many handkerchiefs. 'I know we've got to give this Oriental visitor a warm welcome, but this is ridiculous. It isn't as if he were a Hottentot.'

'Ha, ha,' said the Queen, 'very funny joke, I'm sure. But His Torrid Incandescence the Bunsen-Burnah of Incineratoria comes from a very hot climate. He is accustomed to excessive warmth. And he also has a very fiery and overheated temper. If he feels the slightest bit shivery, he'll declare war just to keep himself warm.'

'Oh dear!' groaned the King, fanning himself with a gas bill. 'Why do we have to invite these highly explosive Eastern gentlemen?'

'It's all a matter of international goodwill,' said the Queen. 'You know that perfectly well. It's like having the neighbours to tea so that they won't complain if you've got the radio on too loud.'

'Well thank goodness our neighbours don't expect us to

live in an overheated greenhouse,' said the King, and he went out for a breath of nice cool fresh air delivered daily straight from the sky, and nothing to pay.

His Torrid Incandescence arrived promptly on time, which was a good thing because if he'd been delayed much the palace would have melted.

'Welcome to Incrediblania!' cried the King. 'Greetings and heatings, and may your temperature never drop below the highest you can stand.'

The Bunsen-Burnah swept into the palace, took off the five fur coats he'd been wearing to keep warm in the not-too-

HIS TORRID INCANDESCENCE THE BUNSEN—BURNAH

sweltering outside climate of Incrediblania, and bowed so low that he nearly scorched his forehead on the floor.

'I am filled with the glowing delights at your so boiling nice welcome,' he said. 'See I bring you the hot stuff entertainments. My own special hotcha-hotcha dancing girls, my imperial fire-eaters, my Superheated Syncopaters, so we all have flaming good time!'

'Well thank goodness he didn't come on droves of elephants that need to be parked and fed and looked after,' whispered the King.

'No,' said the Queen, 'he came in an historic steam engine he bought from British Rail and it's blowing steam and soot all over the garden.'

Then the royal visitor and his hot suite were conducted to the Incrediblanian banqueting hall for a highly Oriental nosh-up.

'I hope he doesn't think we're currying favour with him,' said the King, as steaming helpings of something guaranteed to set your front teeth on fire were handed round.

'Well at least he won't find your jokes any too hot,' said the Queen, putting ice cream on her chillies to cool them.

After the banquet, when the hotcha-hotcha dancers had pranced around until the carpet caught fire and His Torrid Incandescence's Superheated Syncopaters had burned up all the tunes they knew, they all retired to the great hall for refreshments.

Then the head footman sneezed.

Either he'd gone out without his winter woollies, or he hadn't been eating his nice rice pudding, or he must have done something else his mummy had always taught him not to do. Anyway he'd caught a cold and he sneezed.

Well, what's a sneeze among friends? Indeed what is a sneeze even among royal and imperial company?

Well, in this royal and imperial and exceedingly hot-tempered company it was a disaster. His Torrid Incandescence the Bunsen-Burnah of Incineratoria had never heard anyone sneeze. They never did it in his tropical country, and he thought it was rude. He considered it insulting. He felt it was a sauce, and not the peppery sort of sauce he cared for either. And he said so.

'Off with his head!' he cried. 'How dare this insignificant particle of uneatable humanity make this outrageous noise in our august company. Off with his head this minute!'

'No, no, no, no, stop, cease, wait!' cried the King, waving his hands, which caused a draught on the Bunsen-Burnah's face and made him madder than ever. 'You do not understand.'

His Torrid Incandescence went a variety of colours, all of them ferocious.

'It is an insult!' he shouted. 'I will not have the insults. Off with his head this minute, and right off, not just half way. Executioner!' he cried, and a tall figure dressed in black and carrying an enormous axe that looked as if it could open even a tin of baked beans without much difficulty, strode in.

Then Princess Sonia sneezed. So did Princess Rosy. They'd caught a cold through having gone out into the palace private gardens in their bikinis to cool off.

His Torrid Incandescence nearly blew up. Flames would have come out of his ears if they could.

'Now I get the royal insults which are a thousand times worse,' he roared. 'Off with their heads too!'

The two Princesses fainted as gracefully as they could and Prince Poppup and Prince Egbert picked them up. Then the Princes sneezed too because they had caught the Princesses' colds through kissing them.

His Torrid Incandescence thought the royal family were having him on, pulling his leg and taking the mickey. He didn't know any of these expressions, of course, but that's what he thought they were doing.

The Queen rushed up and down the room crying, 'Oh, why ever did we allow this gentleman to come here? You can't execute people for sneezing!' she pleaded with the Incandescence. 'People can't help sneezing.'

'I do not know about the sneezing!' roared His Torridity, turning a repulsive shade of purple with green blotches. 'I do not care who insults me, but I insist that they are executed.'

Oh, dreadful situation! Half the royal family to be executed just to please a ferocious hot-tempered visitor. It was outrageous. No, it was more than outrageous.

Then the King sneezed.

'Ha! So you are in the insulting plot too,' screamed His Torrid Incandescence, giving off fumes like three gas escapes and several bad drains. 'You may be the King of Incrediblania, but you do not insult me. Off with your head too!'

Then sneezing broke out all round the room. His Torrid

Incandescence shouted to the Executioner to get wielding his axe. Pandemonium reigned. There was an uproar. The windows shook. A thunderstorm that was about to start thought better of it and went away. Two earthquakes in a distant land failed to take place, and an eclipse of the sun was cancelled at the last minute.

The Executioner strode forward and brandished his axe, cutting off the lower half of a chandelier, which promptly fell on His Torrid Incandescence's gracious toe and would have made him wilder than ever, but even he couldn't manage to do that.

'Down on your knees and prepare to lose your heads!' he roared. 'And start with him!' He pointed a red-hot finger at the King.

The Executioner grabbed the King. The two Princes rushed to the rescue, but were held back by the Incandescence's guards.

The Executioner pushed the King down on to the floor and swung up his axe.

Then His Torrid Incandescence the Bunsen-Burnah of Incineratoria sneezed.

Oh, wow, yes he did! He'd caught a cold from all the other sneezings.

The Executioner lowered his axe and didn't know what to do.

He wasn't the only one. His Torrid Incandescence changed colour to much cooler and milder shades. His chin dropped, his eyes goggled.

Then he sneezed again, and again, and again.

'Off with his head!' shouted the King, scrambling up. 'Lift up that chopper of yours and get busy on your inflammable master!' he cried. 'He's the distinguished guest. He is entitled to be honoured by being executed first. Ha, ha, get on with it, chop, chop, as I believe they say in some countries.'

The Executioner looked wildly from side to side. He didn't know what to do and would have been scared to do it even if he had known.

'Go on,' shouted the King, 'off with His Torrid Thingummy's head! What do you think you're paid for?'

The Executioner shook his head. He knew what he was paid for, but he hadn't been paid for weeks. His Torridness had forgotten about it and the Executioner dared not remind him or he would have ordered his head off. Though, of course, that would have been silly because there was nobody but the Executioner himself to do it, and how can a man chop off his own head?

The question very nearly answered itself because the Executioner suddenly stopped wagging his head, went, *ah-*, *ah-*, *ah-*, *ah-*, and then sneezed a resounding *tishoo* and dropped his axe, nearly on the King's foot and absolutely on a fancy tea table, which made even more noise than the King would have done.

Good frightfully gracious! Now what a situation! The Executioner, ordered to execute everybody in sight for sneezing, goes and sneezes himself.

'Off with his head!' roared His Torrid Incandescence.

'B-b-b-b-but,' stammered the Executioner, 'I can't chop off my own head. I wouldn't know where to start.'

'That's all right,' said the Queen, handing round fancy coloured tissues, 'the King will do it. Come on, Kingy, pick up that chopper and let's have His Torrid Incandescence's topknot off first, then the Executioner's. After that we needn't bother as there will be nobody's orders left to obey.'

'No, no, no, stop!' cried His Torridness. 'This is absurd.

We cannot all be executed or there will be nobody left to execute anyone.'

'Your Torridness has it all wrong,' said Prince Poppup. 'When we, er, *ah-*, *ah-*, *tishoo!* When we sneeze it isn't meant as an insult. We, *atishoo*, can't help it. It's because we have caught cold.'

'Yes,' put in Princess Sonia, wiping her nose with a piece of fancy lace half an inch square, 'and when someone catches a cold other people catch it from them. That's why we've all been sneezing.'

'And it's your fault really,' said Princess Rosy, borrowing Prince Poppup's handkerchief but, finding that it was full of conkers he had been collecting, she gave it back and took a good royal sniff instead. 'You see it's because we had the palace all hotted and steamed up for you that we caught cold when we went outside.'

His Torrid Incandescence goggled at them. His ears wagged about. 'So it is all, *ah-*, *ah-*, *ah-*, *tishoo*, a mistake,' he sneezed. 'There are no insults. *Atishoo!*'

'A tissue?' said the Queen, handing him two purple and three green ones.

'And you all catch the colds because you hot up the palace for me,' wailed His Torrid Incandescence. 'How can I make amends. I will give you jewels, barrels of them. Diamond necklaces two yards long. Priceless rubies by the dozen, or by the ten if you prefer metric rubies. Gorgeous sapphire thingummies, bundles of exotic ear-rings . . .'

'No, no, no,' cried the Queen, 'please don't! I already have so much jewellery I can't make up my mind what to wear when, and it's very hard work deciding.'

Then Princess Rosy, who wouldn't have minded a cartload or two of jewels herself but couldn't say so after what the

Queen had said, cried, 'I'll get my magic crayons that bring to life whatever I draw with them and draw us a bottle of cold cure. Then we can all take some and be well again.'

She shot upstairs, came back with the crayons, drew an enormous bottle and labelled it 'Instant Cold Cure'.

'I bet it tastes awful,' said the King.

They all took some.

'Phew!' said the King.

'Ouch!' said the Queen.

'Ugh!' said Prince Poppup.

'Ergh!' said Princess Sonia.

'Pwah!' cried Prince Egbert.

'Wurgh!' gurgled Princess Rosy. Then she said, 'Well, anyway, it may not be nice, but it's a nicer cold cure than having your head chopped off, even if it isn't quite as quick!'

Then His Torrid Incandescence took some.

'Ha!' he cried. 'It has the fine bouquet. It tickles the palate. It noses well. *Atishoo!* A handsome vintage. I will have two dozen bottles.'

'He likes it!' said Princess Rosy in amazement.

Everybody's mouth dropped open and they all sneezed at once. The palace windows rattled. The curtains shook.

'Good gracious!' cried the King.

'I forgive the sneezing,' said His Torrid Incandescence. 'You shall supply me with quantities of this delicious nectar and all is well.'

So Incrediblania was safe once more. But Princess Rosy was kept rather busy drawing bottles of her instant cold cure to send to His Torrid Incandescence. And whether it ever cured his cold, or whether he ever caught another one, was never known. But he was delighted and Incrediblania was saved, which was the chief thing that mattered.

2

Triple Trouble for Incrediblania

'I'm very worried,' said the King of Incrediblania, frowning so much that his crown went crooked. 'Everything is much too lovely. Nothing is going wrong.'

'Well, that's nothing to worry about,' said the Queen, who was one of the best worriers in the kingdom as a rule. 'If everything's lovely, there's no need to worry.'

'That sounds very nice,' said the King, 'but I always feel that when everything is as right as it can be, things can only get worse. Any minute now disasters may start taking place. On the other hand, if everything is awful, things can only get better. Oh dear, dear, dear!'

'Well, I'm not going to worry,' said the Queen. 'It isn't as if we were having trouble boiling the eggs for Oriental visitors or having to deal with dragons.'

At that moment there was a knock on the door and in came three dragons. They were the very same dragons who had agreed not to claim the kingdom because the King had let them stay in Incrediblania to have dragon races and be looked after by the wicked Count Bakwerdz.*

'Oh dear,' said the Queen.

'I told you so,' said the King. 'Here comes trouble. Three lots of it with scaly backs and coloured flames.'

'We, um, er, ah,' said the dragons, not blowing out any flames and looking a bit sheepish, which is very difficult for dragons to do.

---

* see *Count Bakwerdz on the Carpet*

'I suppose you're going to demand half the kingdom,' said the King.

'No, no, Your Majesty,' said the first dragon, 'we want to give in our notice.'

'Nonsense!' said the Queen. 'Whoever heard of dragons giving in notice!'

'You just have,' said the second dragon. 'We want to leave.'

'But I thought you liked the dragon races,' said the King.

'Oh, it's not that,' said dragon number three. 'No, it's Count Bakwerdz's cooking. We can't stand it.'

'Hard-boiled lettuce,' said dragon number one. 'Even vegetarians like us draw the line at that.'

'Underdone potatoes,' said dragon two, 'hard as cannon balls.'

'Burnt carrots,' said dragon three. 'They taste awful.'

'Perhaps we could get you a better cook,' suggested the King. But the dragons said no, they were tired of Incrediblania anyway and wanted to go somewhere else for a change. So off they went with wings swishing and tails waving.

'Ah, ha, good riddance,' growled the wicked Count Bakwerdz, sweeping vegetables out of his grim, grey castle and throwing them over into the next door garden. 'I'm glad to be rid of them. Now I can start plotting to seize the kingdom again.'

Back at the palace the Queen was saying she didn't see what there was to worry about now.

'The dragons have gone,' she said, 'and even though they gave no trouble while they were here, I was always afraid they might start.'

But the King kept on worrying. He was sure something

frightful was going to happen. And he was most considerably right.

Three days after the dragons had left, there came a sound like several assorted thunderstorms accompanied by a young earthquake. The earth trembled. The people of Incrediblania trembled even more. And soon it was the turn of the King and Queen to tremble. Usually whatever was done the King and Queen did it first, but trembling was the last thing they wanted to do.

Then the door of the palace opened and a hand the size of two sideboards came in, picked up the King and pulled him outside. In the courtyard stood a giant; an absolute whopper

he was with a black beard, a red nose and green eyes.

He put the King down and said in a voice that could be heard two kingdoms away without any microphones, 'You're King of this joint, aren't you? Well, I'm going to live here and you're going to feed me, otherwise I bash the place up, got it?' He stamped one foot slightly and the Queen's second best summerhouse fell down, just as Princess Sonia was about to have tea in it.

'Now, now, now, what's all this?' demanded the Queen, coming out into the courtyard.

'I'm a telling of your little husband, M'm,' said the giant, 'that he's got to keep me in food or I smash up your kingdom, so there!'

'Nonsense,' said the Queen, sticking her nose in the air, which she had to do to see the giant, although she always did that anyway when speaking to people she felt beneath her. 'Nonsense,' she repeated. 'Aren't you supposed to say fee, fi, fo, fum, or something?'

'Ah, that's old hat,' growled the giant. 'But I mean what I say. I'm going back to me home in the hills and I want me meals regular. You won't find it too bad. I'm not a big eater. Just twenty-five eggs for breakfast with six loaves nicely toasted and washed down with five gallons of tea, and don't forget the sugar.'

'Er, no, we won't forget that,' said the King.

'Then for lunch a nice roast ox, a cake two feet square for tea—not too much so as not to spoil me supper. Shall we say ten chickens, a couple of geese and five barrels of ale for that? Well, I'll be off, and don't forget I likes me meals punctual *or else* . . .' He pulled up an oak tree by its roots, snapped off the branches and strode away, swinging the tree like a huge club.

'Oh, my goodness!' gasped the Queen. 'Whatever are we to do? We can't keep feeding him or we'll have no food left for anyone else.'

'If only the dragons hadn't left,' cried the King. 'They could have dealt with him even though they were vegetarians.'

'Well, we could send out a proclamation to get someone to kill the giant,' said the Queen. 'There's no nonsense about half the kingdom reward for doing that.'

'No,' said the King, 'and no chance of anyone trying to do it either with a chap that size.'

'I reckon as I could do it,' cried an enormous voice, sounding like five prize brass bands, and another giant with a red beard, a blue nose and yellow eyes this time stepped over the palace wall.

'Good gracious, another giant!' cried the Queen. 'I don't believe it.'

'You don't 'ave to, M'm,' said the giant. 'I ain't a giant, I'm a hogre.'

'He means an ogre,' whispered the King.

'Yus thut's right, a hogre,' said the ogre. 'Hi be a hogre.'

'Oh dear,' said the Queen, 'if he keeps putting "h"s where they shouldn't be, I hope he doesn't go dropping them too. From his height they might hurt someone.'

'What's the difference between a giant and an ogre anyway?' asked the Minister of Information, coming cautiously out of a side door.

'A giant eats things like cattle,' said the Court Magician, putting his head out of a window. 'An ogre eats people.'

'Oh!' shrieked the Queen.

'Ah, ha!' growled the ogre. 'Now I be willing to eat that giant of yours, if you promise to keep me in regular meals. A few nice juicy young maidens for breakfast, say, and . . .'

'No, no, no, no!' cried the King. 'This is too much. First we get dragons, but they eat only vegetables, then we get a giant who eats meat, now we've got an ogre who eats people. What are we to do?'

'You just say the word and I'll deal wiv your giant,' said the ogre. 'Then you can send me up a nice supper of plump young men. But if yer don't,' and he shook a carving knife three yards long, 'I'll kick down your palace and houses and eat everyone up. Be seeing yer,' and with that he stamped off after the giant.

'This is awful,' groaned the King. 'If we let him eat the giant, he'll eat everyone else in the kingdom as well. And besides the giant might kill him first, so we're for it anyway.'

Up in the hills the giant and the ogre were laughing like five thunderstorms.

'I told 'em I eat people,' said Red Beard. 'Said I was a hogre I did. Course I don't eat people, but they didn't know that. Didn't 'alf scare 'em I can tell you. Reckon as they'll give me anything I want now to stop me eating 'em, ha, ha!'

'Ho, very funny,' said Black Beard, suddenly not laughing, 'but I heard you telling that king as you'd eat me as long as he gave you what you wanted. Don't you go trying that on, or I might kill you. Anyway if you was to eat people there'd be nobody to bring food up to me, so you look out.'

Just then who should appear from behind a rock but the wicked Count Bakwerdz, waving a white handkerchief that was supposed to be a flag of truce.

'Hist,' he hissed.

'What say?' said the giants.

'Let us get together,' said the wicked Count. 'I have a plan to benefit us all. Listen.' He turned to Red Beard. 'You go

22

down and eat the King and Queen and the ministers. Then I can claim the throne and rule the kingdom.'

'What's the good of that to us?' growled the giants.

'Why, once I'm in command,' said the Count, 'I can send you up all you want in the way of food and even have a castle built for you. You can live in luxury. I'll be glad to have you to scare dragons away.'

'Right,' said the giants, 'let's get the details settled.' And the three of them began to talk.

Down at the palace everybody didn't know what to do.

'If the Court Magician still has some of his magic ferti-lizer,' said the Queen, 'we could quickly grow a giant bean-stalk and cut it down as the giants climbed down it.'

'We'd have to get them to climb up it first,' said the King, 'and I don't see how we can do that.'

'How about digging a pit for them to fall into,' said the Minister of Agriculture, who didn't dig anything except funny music.

'To dig a hole big enough so that those giants couldn't climb out of it would take about five years,' said the Prime Minister, who'd once spent all day trying to dig up a determined weed.

'Pity those three dragons left,' said the Lord Chancellor. Then he left himself as it was time for his tea-break.

Up in the hills the wicked Count Bakwerdz was still plot-ting. Red Beard had got tired of listening and had fallen asleep.

'Come over here,' whispered the Count to Black Beard. 'There's no need to let him in on this. He promised the King he'd eat you, you know, and he might try. Why don't you write him off while he's asleep, then you and I can seize the kingdom and have it all to ourselves.'

'Cor, yes, not arf!' said Black Beard. 'I'll go and get me club.'

The wicked Count crept craftily away and hid under a rock.

The 'How to Deal with the Giants' conference was still going on at the palace, but nobody had thought of anything. Then suddenly it became dark.

'Don't say we have a power cut,' groaned the King. 'As if we haven't enough troubles already.'

'We can't have a power cut,' said the Queen. 'We don't have any power.'

But it wasn't a power cut. It was an extra large, super family-sized dragon flying overhead.

'Oh, my goodness!' cried everyone, rushing out and staring up at the huge dark mass in the sky.

'He doesn't look as if he'd be a vegetarian like our other ones,' said the Queen nervously.

'What a monster!' cried the King. 'What with him and the giants, we've really had it.'

'Call out the Artillery!' commanded the Defence Minister. 'Shoot it down!'

'Not on my rose garden!' shrieked the Queen.

'Mind my greenhouses!' yelled the King.

The Artillery came rushing out with their guns. They pointed them up at the dragon and fired. But by then the dragon was too far away and all they did was knock a few scales off his tail.

'Perhaps he'll go away now,' said the King hopefully, but not expecting it.

And just then the huge dragon wheeled round, and made another run over the palace.

Up in the hills the most terrific fight was going on between the giants. *Bang, crash, wallop, growl, roar, thump.* 'Gotcher!' ' 'Ave at yer!'

Behind the rock the wicked Count Bakwerdz was gloating away at full revs.

'Ha, ha, ha,' he gloated, which is a bit difficult to do, but he managed it. 'One of them will settle the other, then I can get the one who's left to deal with the King and the ministers and I'll take over the country.'

Bang, thud, roar, the fight between the giants went on. Then suddenly a cloud appeared in the sky. But it wasn't a cloud, it was the enormous dragon. And it was in a dragon of a temper too. So would you be if you'd had scales shot off your tail as he had.

'Grrrrr,' roared the dragon. Then he saw the two giants fighting below. With another roar he swooped down. He grabbed the giant in one huge claw and the ogre in the other. Count Bakwerdz dashed out from behind his rock, cheering like mad.

'Hu-, jolly well, -rray!' he cried. 'The dragon is carrying off both giants. Now I can go down and claim a reward for saving the kingdom from the giants. Nobody will know it wasn't I who did it. In fact I'll claim the throne and the whole kingdom, because I can say if it wasn't for me the giants would have destroyed everything.'

But, aha, to use a favourite expression of the Count's, he'd gloated too soon, which is always silly. The Count had counted on too much, which is even sillier, because just then the dragon swooped down and snatched up the wicked

Count firmly by his braces and flew off.

But ha! Or ooer! Or wow! The Count's braces snapped. They were very cheap ones, as the Count was too mean to buy good ones. Down he fell. Down and down, splash into a lake. The dragon flew off with the giants, and the Count crawled sopping wet out of the lake.

The 'How to Deal with the Giants' conference at the palace had now changed to 'How to Deal with the Dragon'. And everybody had just as many ideas about this, as they had for dealing with the giants, that is to say, none at all.

Then in at the door came Count Bakwerdz, still sopping wet and with a surprised frog sitting on top of his head.

'I have destroyed the giants,' he cried, 'and I claim half the kingdom as a reward!'

'There's no half kingdom reward for killing *giants*,' said the King.

'Ah, ha!' cried the Count. 'But I rid the kingdom of the dragon too, so you do owe me half the kingdom.'

Good gracious! Was the wicked Count going to get away with it?

No, thank goodness, for at that moment Princess Sonia and Prince Egbert came dashing in. 'Arrest him!' cried the Prince, waving a telescope and busting half a chandelier. 'We were watching from the tower to see what the giants were doing and we saw exactly what happened.'

He explained to the King how the dragon had flown off with the giants, and how it would have taken the wicked Count too, if his braces hadn't snapped.

'It's a pity you don't wear decent braces,' said the King to the Count. 'It's a disgrace for a man in your position to have such cheap ones. But since they let you down and saved you from the dragon, perhaps its lucky for you, though not for us. But as for half the kingdom, all the kingdom you're going to get is a whole dungeon.'

'Oh, no!' sneered the Count. 'I may not be able to claim half the kingdom, but at least I helped to get rid of the giants, so I deserve some reward.'

He hadn't really of course. It was the enormous dragon who had got rid of the giants. But you can't very well give a reward to an enormous dragon who isn't there any more.

'Oh, all right,' said the King, 'you can go back and live in your grim, grey castle and we'll give you a small reward for your pains.'

So the wicked Count went back to his grim, grey castle and gloated so much over his reward he gave himself hiccoughs.

But the reward the King gave him was a shiny silver lamp that took no end of cleaning. That kept the Count so busy he didn't have time to plot any more wickednesses for quite a while.

3
Royal D.I.Y.

The Queen of Incrediblania was looking through her diary to see if anything nice and enjoyable, such as a tremendous banquet, or a presentation from grateful subjects, or an exotic summer holiday, was due to happen shortly.

She found none of these things, but what she did find was that Their Majesties the King and Queen of Crashbania were coming on a state visit very soon.

'Oh, my goodness!' she cried. She dashed in to the King, who was busy doing nothing at all, and stopped him.

'Royal visitors are coming next week!' she cried, waving her hands and making an awful draught. 'We must get the drawing-room redecorated.'

'Must we?' muttered the King. 'I thought we had it done after those three dragons mucked it up.'

'That was the great hall,' said the Queen and she stopped waving her hands as the draught had made her hair-do go a bit shaggy. 'The drawing-room hasn't been done for ages. Give orders to have it repainted and repapered and re-whatever else is needed. I don't want the Queen of Crashbania to think we live all slummy.'

The King didn't quite see how even a queen could think it slummy to have a drawing-room with five chandeliers, nine gilt couches and enormous paintings by world-famous artists, most of whom were dead, which meant their paintings were all the more valuable.

'That's going to be a bit difficult,' he said. 'The royal decorators are on holiday and they won't be back in time.'

'Oh dear!' wailed the Queen. 'Now what are we going to do? The Crashbanians have the most utterly luxurious palace with double glazing, insulated cavity walls, illuminated ceilings and two bathrooms to every bedroom.'

'How ghastly!' groaned the King, who didn't like having baths much, because he rather hated getting out of the nice hot water.

'Aren't there people who do this sort of thing by post?' asked the Queen. 'Or can't we get the Army to do it instead of marching up and down stamping up dust and shouting commands so that I can't hear the gossip Cousin Rona is telling me.'

'We can't let the Army in,' said the King. 'They'd try to shoot down cobwebs and make pincer movements on the walls. And I've never heard of drawing-rooms being decorated by post, though, of course, if you tell your painters to do it you are sort of directing males.'

This last joke was so complicated even the King couldn't see it himself. But he suddenly saw something else.

'I see this', he said, 'as a chance to express myself artistically. I shall redecorate the drawing-room myself. Er, with the help of the ministers, of course.'

'Pah!' snorted the Queen. 'The last time you expressed yourself artistically you painted a lot of frightful pictures and people who came to see them in the gallery bought the "No Smoking" and "Exit" notices instead!'

'All right,' said the King, 'but this is different. Painting pictures is hard because you have to do perspective and fearsome things like that. Decorating a room is easy. You just slap the paint on the walls or stick the paper on and so forth. If mere painters can do it, why can't I?'

The Queen thought that as far as decorating the drawing-room was concerned the painters were likely to be a lot less mere than the King and the ministers. But all she said was, 'Well I don't like the idea, but there's no help for it. The Crashbanians will be here next week and they mustn't see the drawing-room in its present state. It isn't the sort of state a state apartment should be in.'

The King didn't laugh because the Queen hadn't laughed at his joke. He shot off to round up the ministers and get paint and wallpaper and ladders and brushes and things organized.

'First of all I shall decide on the colour scheme,' said the Queen.

That would have taken longer than waiting for the royal painters to get back from holiday, but the King said, 'No time for that, we'll just redo it the same colour as before.' So the Queen went off to decide on new colour schemes for wardrobesful of new dresses instead.

The redecorating of the royal drawing-room was raging with panic-stricken high speed.

'Don't waste a second!' panted the King, stirring paint as if he were trying to make it into a milk shake. 'Their Crashbanian Majesties will be here in a few days.'

'Right, full speed ahead!' cried the First Sea Lord, who was up the top of a tall ladder, which was a change from a ship's mast.

The Lord Chancellor and the Lord Chamberlain were busy scraping off the wallpaper, because you have to do this before you put new wallpaper on, otherwise it all falls off in untidy coils. Goodness knows how they knew that, but perhaps it was one of the laws of Incrediblania.

The carpets had been taken up, the chandeliers had been

taken down and the servants were taken by surprise at having to keep bringing in cups of tea to the King and the ministers to keep their strength up.

Slap, slop, went the paint brushes. *Snip, snip*, went the wall-paper scissors. *Slosh, slosh*, went the paste. The King and the Lord Chancellor collided in the middle of the ladder and were enveloped in highly expensive royal wallpaper. The Lord Chief Justice got one long piece of wallpaper nicely spread out and smoothed down just in time to find it was upside down.

The Minister for the Interior, after he'd got paint on his eyebrows and wallpaper paste on his trousers, decided this wasn't the kind of interior he really wanted to minister to.

'This is more difficult than ruling the kingdom, but rather more fun,' said the King, sloshing a brushful of paste into the Lord Chancellor's face.

The Lord Chief Justice said longer and more severe sentences than he ever did in court.

'How are you getting on?' asked the Queen through the keyhole of the ante-room, as she wasn't going to risk going inside the room in case she got paint on her face.

'Nearly finished!' cried the King, taking a ladder away and leaving the First Sea Lord clinging to an ornamental cupid on the ceiling. Then the other ministers had to hold out a dust-sheet as if they were firemen with a jumping sheet. The First Sea Lord came down *whizzzzz, bong*, into it, raising dust that clung itself lovingly to the wet paint and they had to do that bit over again.

'Hurry up!' shouted the Queen through the keyhole. Then she went away to have a nice quiet cup of tea, because she felt rather exhausted at all the hard work the King and the ministers were doing.

*

At last the work of redecorating the royal drawing-room was finished. The mess was almost cleaned up, the dust-sheets and ladders were taken away, and the King and ministers took off their overalls.

'There you are,' said the King, as he took the Queen in to see the result of their work. 'All done in good time and not bad, I think.'

'*Not bad!*' shrieked the Queen. 'I should say it isn't bad. It's terrible!'

And it was. The wallpaper was crooked, there was paint on the gilt mirrors where it shouldn't have been, and the ceiling looked like a photo of the craters of the moon.

'Oh, my goodness!' cried the Queen.

'Well, we did our best in the time allowed,' said the King.

'I don't care what you did,' said the Queen, stamping up and down in a royal rage. 'Even if you'd done it beautifully, it would still be terrible.'

'How could it be terrible, if it was beautiful?' said the King.

'Because', said the Queen, standing very still, folding her arms and giving the King a look like a ten-yard corkscrew, 'you've redecorated the wrong room.'

'What!' squeaked the King and the ministers. And the First Sea Lord went out to let off steam at the sailors.

'You've decorated the blue drawing-room,' said the Queen. 'It was the white drawing-room I wanted done.'

'How was I to know that?' asked the King.

'Because we always use the white drawing-room to entertain visiting royalty,' said the Queen. 'You know that perfectly well. We only use the blue drawing-room when Auntie Judy is coming to visit, because blue is her favourite colour.

Blues are her favourite music, she has blue blood in her veins, blue eyes and she's rather a blue stocking, being very intellectual.'

'Well there's no need for you to scream blue murder,' said the King. 'We can still entertain the King and Queen of Crashbania in the white drawing-room.'

'We shall have to,' said the Queen. 'It may be a bit mucky judged by royal standards, but at least it's better than this imperial infliction, this regal rubbish, this royal razzle-dazzle.'

'Stop talking like a poet,' said the King. 'We'll get the servants to clean up the white drawing-room as best they can and hope the Crashbanians won't notice too much.'

'Queen Margaret of Crashbania wears very strong spectacles,' said the Queen. 'She can spot a speck of dust at ten yards and see a crooked picture five rooms away. But we shall have to hope for the best, that's all.'

The day of the royal Crashbanian visit arrived dead on time. The red carpet was laid without any mishaps. Count Bakwerdz was carefully kept out of the way, locked in his grim, grey castle where he could gloat as much as he liked, which he didn't like much because he couldn't plot any dastardly plans. The Royal Incrediblanian Guards turned out, looking tremendously smart with their hats on the right way round, their buttons polished almost out of existence and their faces washed right round to the backs of their necks. The Crashbanian state coach came clop, clopping along with a sound like coconut shells being banged on a board. The Incrediblanian Band played the Crashbanian National Anthem and got it all right by accident.

'Welcome to Incrediblania!' said the King, as the King

and Queen of Crashbania gracefully stepped out of their coach.

'How nice of you to have the sun shining,' said the Queen of Crashbania in her best party voice.

'Nice little place you have here,' grunted the King of Crashbania, looking at the royal palace which was about the size of ten cinemas and three bingo halls.

Then the royal party went inside and were conducted with much bowing and curtseying up stairs, along corridors, round corners, through ante-rooms and into the white drawing-room.

'I do hope you'll excuse the dreadful state of this room,' said the Queen of Incrediblania, 'but the decorators are on holiday, you know.'

The King of Crashbania looked at a dirty patch on the wall where the King of Incrediblania's nephew had written something impolite and tried to rub it out before his uncle saw it.

'I'd just like to have a look at her kitchen,' whispered the Queen of Crashbania to the King. 'If her drawing-room is like this, goodness knows what her stove looks like.'

Just then Princess Rosy and her husband Prince Poppup, and Princess Sonia with her husband Prince Egbert arrived looking rather pink because they'd been held up in a traffic jam.

'So sorry we're, puff, puff, a bit late,' gasped Princess Sonia.

'But better late than never,' said Princess Rosy.

'And all's well that ends well,' put in Prince Egbert, who thought if they were talking proverbs he might as well say one.

'I say, you know,' said Prince Poppup, looking round the

room, 'we really ought to have had this place done up a bit for Their Majesties' visit, oughtn't we? I mean it looks a bit, er, er . . .'

'Mucky,' said Princess Sonia, 'but the decorators are on holiday and Daddy redecorated the blue drawing-room by mistake.'

'Indeed,' said the Queen of Crashbania, looking at everyone through a pair of spectacles on the end of a stick, 'then pray let us adjourn to the blue drawing-room if that is less, er, mucky.'

'But . . .' began the King.

He was too late. The royal party swept out of the white drawing-room. They swept back along corridors, round corners, through ante-rooms and into the blue drawing-room.

'Dear me,' said the Queen of Crashbania, 'if you called the other room mucky, what kind of word would you use for this?'

'I know it's frightful,' stammered the King of Incrediblania, 'but as the decorators were on holiday I did the job myself, assisted by my ministers. I'm afraid,' he added, 'we aren't very good at this do-it-yourself lark.'

The King of Crashbania clapped him on the back and knocked his crown off.

'Don't worry,' he cried, 'the do-it-yourself thing is my hobby. Now that we are here, pray allow me to help you and your ministers redecorate the white drawing-room. We can then go on to do this room.'

'With your kind help we can do both at once!' cried the King of Incrediblania, coming over all excited. 'The ladies can sit in the great hall and have tea and talk gossip while we do it.'

Good gracious! What an impossible, imperial situation.

Two kings about to redecorate drawing-rooms? Whatever next!

'It's very kind of your husband to help Montgomery decorate the drawing-rooms,' said the Queen of Incrediblania to the Queen of Crashbania as they sat regally and chummily in the great hall, enjoying gossip, tea and cream buns together.

'Well, I only hope he doesn't make a mess of it,' said the Queen of Crashbania. 'Do you know,' she leant forward and her diamond necklace dipped in her tea, but didn't make it taste any nicer, 'he once tried to turn one of the bathrooms into a cinema so that he could watch Sophia Loren while he was having a bath. Most unsuitable, I thought.'

'Ah well, kings will be boys,' said the Queen of Incrediblania, 'but I do hope they'll make a better job of it than Monty did of the blue drawing-room. We've got a very touchy Oriental potentate coming to visit in a week or so and it's awkward enough having technicolour elephants in the palace yard getting all mixed up with the changing of the guard, without having to explain why the royal drawing-room looks like a British Rail station after a visit by football fans.'

Days went by. In the royal drawing-rooms the two Kings, in special overalls with their respective royal arms embroidered on them, were sploshing and pasting away, helped by the ministers. In no time at all the white drawing-room was stripped out and the blue drawing-room was done over, and, after a considerably little more time, the white drawing-room was redecorated.

'There you are, my dear,' said both Kings at once, coming

in rubbing their hands, 'both rooms done and all ready.'

But when the Queen of Incrediblania saw them she fainted three times in five seconds and had to be brought round with chocolate cake and almond slices.

'This is terrible!' she gasped. 'Terribler than before. You've wrecked both rooms. And that quick-tempered Oriental gentleman's coming on a state visit next week. Oh! Oh! We're undone!'

It certainly looked like it. The white drawing-room now looked nine and a half times worse than the blue drawing-room had looked after the King had decorated it. And the blue drawing-room now looked several decimal fractions worse.

'The potentate will be furious,' wailed the Queen of Incrediblania, while the Queen of Crashbania had a piece of chocolate cake herself to keep her courage up. 'There will be war over this, I know there will. Oh! I wish I wasn't a Queen. I wish I was one of those ladies who have a nice quiet job making appointments for people to see the dentist. If an Oriental potentate happens to visit them, he's the one who has to worry.'

But oh! What Incrediblanian luck! The disaster was averted by two dabs of wallpaper paste and half a pint of blue paint. The royal decorators arrived back from holiday in the nick of time, which fortunately was a fairly large nick that particular year. And the King paid them extra to work like mad and get the two drawing-rooms redone and looking regal again in time for the potentate's visit.

But the potentate sent a message saying he couldn't come after all, as his best elephant had a corn and couldn't walk.

4

King Jan the First

'I', said the King of Incrediblania, 'am going to make a New Year Resolution. A mind-boggling, eyebrow-raising, smack-on-the-chin resolution. I am going to resign.'

'You're going to what?' gasped the Queen.

'No, I'm not going to what,' said the King. 'I'm going to resign, abdi-what's-its-name.'

'But you can't,' said the Queen. 'It's not consti-thingummy.'

'I don't care what it's not,' said the King. 'With all this plotting by the wicked Count Bakwerdz trying to steal the throne, I'm going to resign and we're going to draw lots among the ministers and myself to see who is to be King. Then, whether I'm chosen or not, nobody can say the Count ought to be King, not even him. Of course,' he went on, 'if one of the ministers becomes King, I shall still be in the background to advise.'

'You needn't bother,' said the Queen. 'I shall still be Queen and I'll do all the advising necessary.'

'Um,' said the King, secretly rather hoping he didn't get chosen and feeling a bit sorry for the minister who did.

They called the Royal Poet and told him to write out the names of the King and all the ministers on slips of paper for the draw.

'Print them, don't write them,' said the Queen. 'Nobody can read your writing and then we'd never know who was King.'

So the Royal Poet went away, carefully tore up some strips

of paper, printed the names of the King and the ministers one on each piece, folded them and put them into a box.

'Aha, ha, ha,' gloated the wicked Count Bakwerdz, having his best gloat for years, when he heard the news. 'Now this really is a chance I never expected. I have a plan, a plot, a scheme. I shall get myself chosen. I know I'm not a minister and shouldn't be in the draw, but if my name is drawn out I'll be King and they can't stop me. That's the rule.' And he went gloating away to plot his plan.

The day of the Great Royal Draw arrived, and tremendous crowds surrounded the palace. All the ministers were assembled, some hoping to become King and some hoping not to, because they were rather scared of the Queen.

'I am graciously pleased to let the draw be made,' said the King, putting on his royal voice good and heavy in case it was the last time he got the chance.

The Royal Poet came forward with the box containing the slips of paper. He put it on a table. He pulled up his sleeves as if he were going to do a conjuring trick. He shut his eyes. He put his hand into the box and pulled out a slip of paper.

'Who is it? Who is it?' gasped everyone. Eyes came out on stalks. Breath came extra bated. Duchesses would have fainted, only they didn't want to miss anything.

The Royal Poet unfolded the paper and read out.

'The new King of Incrediblania is Johnny Smith.'

A gasp went up from the crowd that sounded like all the world's gas leaks.

'Johnny Smith!' cried the King. 'He's not a minister, he's my nephew.'

'Viscount John of Incrediblania,' said the Queen, 'that's his real name, but they call him Johnny Smith at school

because it's easier. But I don't see how he can be King, he's only ten and he isn't a minister.'

'By the royal rules,' said the King, 'whoever's name is drawn must become King. I don't know how Johnny's name got in here, but King he must be and I suggest he be called King Jan the First, to commemorate my New Year Resolution.'

But what had happened? Was this the wicked Count

Bakwerdz's crafty plot to become King? If so it had backfired, blown a fuse and bust a gasket.

Ha. Yes, it was and yes, it had.

The wicked Count had gone to the Royal Poet as he was printing out the names, and, while pretending to help him with his spelling, had stolen some of the paper he was using. Then he'd printed his own name on the slips he made from it and put them into a box just like the one the Poet was using, which was easy because it was one of the Queen's old shoe-boxes and the palace was littered with them as she bought shoes as often as other people buy chocolates.

Then, while the Poet was having his tea-break, the Count put his box in place of the real one.

'Ah, ha,' he gloated, 'now whatever slip is chosen, it's bound to be one with my name on it.'

But wait! Stop a minute! Hold on! Whoa! How did the King's nephew's name come to be chosen then? It wasn't in the box.

Oh, yes it was.

The paper the Poet was printing the names on was torn from an exercise book belonging to the King's nephew, which he'd only partly filled before getting moved up to another class. And he'd printed his name at the top of each page. The Count, so busy gloating over his wicked plot, didn't notice it and so one of the slips he tore off had the King's nephew's name on it and not the Count's.

Johnny Smith, or rather King Jan the First, was delighted.

'No more school!' he cried. 'No more homework. I can do as I like, have lots of fun. Wow! Fancy me being King. Whizzo!'

The Court was in a fluster. Royal banquets were all upside down with various kinds of pudding being served as ten of the twelve courses. Lemonade was served instead of wine. People who had to be knighted got such a wallop with the sword from King Jan the First they fell over, and some were too fat to get up, even though they weren't wearing armour.

The wicked Count Bakwerdz was furious. Smoke came out of his ears. He would have breathed fire, if he'd known how to.

'Hist, boy,' he growled into the new King's ear. 'You're not supposed to be King. That's the job I'd planned for myself. Now you make the laws I tell you, or else.' And he waved a long sharp dagger.

King Jan the First parked a piece of bubble gum on the dagger and said in what he thought was a kingly voice,

'On the con-thingummy,' he said, 'you will do as I tell you or I shall expose you.'

'Ha, you can't,' snarled the Count.

'Oh yes, I can,' said King Jan. 'I found out that all those other papers in the box had your name on. If Uncle knew that, he'd have you thrown into the dungeons. He'd probably have to have you executed, though he doesn't like doing things like that. But the law says if anyone plots to usurp the throne, he shall lose his head.'

'Pah!' snorted the Count, losing his temper instead.

'Now,' said King Jan, popping a toffee into his mouth and wagging a finger as he'd seen the Queen do to the King when she was ordering him about, 'you, glug, pwouff, glug,' he chewed up the toffee and went on, 'you jolly well do exactly as I say, or you're for it.'

The wicked Count slunk away. He was beaten again. And this time by a schoolboy of ten. Oh, the disgrace!

'It's a good job the Poet picked my name instead of the Count's,' said King Jan to himself.

But the Count's plot was discovered anyway because the Royal Poet found his name on all the other slips when he was tidying up and emptying the box that had been used for the draw. So Count Bakwerdz went back into the dungeons and the dungeon guards had to be given a rise to make up for it.

But everything wasn't all right even then.

King Jan the First began to find being King wasn't such fun as he thought.

Although he didn't have to go to school, he had so many state documents to sign they were worse than homework.

Then he had to keep opening bazaars, laying foundation

stones and attending meetings, all of which he found a crashing bore.

Wherever he went, he was accompanied by guards and equerries and officials of all kinds.

And every time he went anywhere, the National Anthem of Incrediblania was played and he had to stand still like everyone else until it finished. And it took no end of a time.

So he went along to his uncle the ex-King.

'Please, Uncle,' he said, 'I don't want to be King. I'd rather go back to school and be Johnny Smith again. This ruling business isn't as much fun as I thought it would be.'

'Ha, ha! You see,' said the King. 'But I don't think you can get out of it. Having one king abdicate is a bit much, I must admit, even though I did it myself. But to have two kings ducking out one after the other. Dear me, no. Whatever would people say?'

'Nothing of the kind,' said a voice that sounded like a small hurricane blowing round shaky chimneys. And the Queen swept in.

'I always said this New Year Resolution of yours was a mistake,' she said to the ex-King. 'It could easily have been a New Year Revolution, if the wicked Count had been chosen as he'd plotted to be. There's no need for any fuss. Johnny can just resign in favour of his uncle and you can be King again. I shall be graciously pleased to be only too pleased. You're a great deal easier, to, er, to, um, er . . .'

'Boss about,' said Johnny.

'Shall we say Keep in Order,' said the Queen, sticking her nose in the air. 'Order the heralds to announce that King Jan the First has resigned and his uncle will once more rule the kingdom. Under my instructions,' she added, 'but don't tell them to say that.'

So the New Year in Incrediblania went on all right in spite of its rather drastic start. And the wicked Count was back in the dungeons. But not for long, because the dungeon guards threatened to resign like the King if he stayed there.

5

A Neighbourly Affair

The Head Gardener of Incrediblania came carefully into the palace, wiped his boots for five minutes, bowed low to the King and Queen and said,

'Oi thought as ow oi should tell ee, Your Majesties, as someone do be a throwing of weeds and rubbish over your garden wall like. It be those folk in Farrawania.'

'Do it now? Er, I mean does it or is it?' said the King. 'Well I'm not having the Farrawanians using Incrediblania as a rubbish heap. You just go and throw it all back.'

'And while you're about it,' said the Queen, 'you can throw over any weeds and rubbish of ours that we want to get rid of, just to teach them.'

'Oh, ah, Your Majesty,' said the Head Gardener, and he went out without wiping his boots as they were now clean and, anyway, it doesn't matter if you tread dirt into the garden.

The Incrediblanian gardeners had no sooner thrown the rubbish and weeds over into Farrawania than the Farrawanians threw it back. Then the Incrediblanians returned it with a bit added, the Farrawanians retaliated with hedge clippings and rotten apples, to which the Incrediblanians countered with grass cuttings, dandelions and stinging nettles.

A few days later there was a trumpet call outside the palace of Incrediblania. Guards stamped their feet and presented arms. Twenty-one guns were fired. The red carpet

was laid out and in strode the King of Farrawania.

'Here, I say, you know,' he said, taking his crown off and hanging it on a vase, which fell on to the floor but didn't break, thank goodness, 'this won't do, you know. You can't go throwing weeds and rubbish into my kingdom.'

'Can't we?' said the King. 'I think we can. In fact I think we do it rather well.'

'It's not royal,' said the King of Farrawania. 'Neither is it neighbourly. Please have it stopped.'

'Not until you stop having weeds and rubbish thrown into our kingdom,' said the Queen.

The King of Farrawania gasped. 'You don't mean', he said, 'that my people are throwing rubbish into your garden?'

'That's exactly what we do mean,' said the Queen, 'and if you'll kindly stop them doing it, we'll stop our gardeners from throwing it back.'

'In fact, if your gardeners don't throw weeds and rubbish in the first place, we can't throw it back,' said the King. 'That's logical.'

'Done,' said the King of Farrawania. 'I will give orders to stop all this rubbish-throwing and we can be friends.'

They all shook hands. Tea and cakes were brought in, caused to disappear without the aid of magic, and the King of Farrawania went home again.

'Whatever is that frightful row?' cried the Queen, rushing about with her hands over her ears, which did a bit of no-good to her hair-do.

'Please, Your Majesty,' said the Lord Chamberlain, 'it is the Queen of Farrawania's nephew practising the trumpet.'

'Oh, is it,' said the Queen. 'Well, two can play at that kind of musical game. Go and tell the King's nephew to take his record player down to the wall next to the Farrawanian palace and play his loudest record.'

'But, Majesty,' protested the Lord Chamberlain, 'that will only make the noise worse, with two of them at it, I mean.'

'You should know better than to argue with me,' said the Queen. And the Lord Chamberlain did, so he went to find the King's nephew and soon the sound of trumpet-practising from Farrawania was almost drowned by the sound of disco music from Incrediblania. Nobody could hear themselves speak and most didn't try.

Presently a new noise was added to the tumult. It was the sound of another twenty-one gun salute and the stamping of guards' feet and the clash of presenting arms as the Queen of Farrawania swept in.

'I won't have it!' she cried. 'It's more than we royalty can be expected to bear. Revolutions, possibly, they're an occupational hazard. Dragons, perhaps, because they're indigi-what's-its-name. Petitions, parades and pretentious public pomp and pageantry, very likely. Foundation stone-laying and bazaar-opening, inevitably. But loud disco music, no. No, no, a whatever number of times it is, no.'

'Do have a cup of coffee and one of my home-made cakes,' said the Queen of Incrediblania, who hadn't heard a word because of the din outside.

'I said we can't put up with that awful record,' shouted the Queen of Farrawania.

'I'm sorry I can't hear you because of that frightful trumpet your nephew is playing,' said the Queen of Incrediblania.

At last, by writing down what they wanted to say and passing messages to and fro, the two Queens found out what they were trying to say to each other.

'Oh Jannie's disco music,' said the Queen of Incrediblania. 'Awful, isn't it? I'm so glad you can't stand it. We can't stand it ourselves. Neither can we stand that trumpet-blowing of your nephew's. That's why we told Jannie to play his records.'

'Pah!' snorted the Queen of Farrawania, tossing her head and making her false eyelashes go crooked. 'You just stop your Jannie from playing his records and we'll stop my nephew from blowing his own trumpet. Goodness knows, his father does enough of that.'

So the two Queens shook hands, had cups of coffee and home-made cakes, and all was well.

'I must say,' said the King of Incrediblania afterwards, 'that between us we've managed these situations most diplo-whateveritis.'

That same afternoon they were taking royal tea in the royal rose garden when up from the next-door kingdom came a line of washing like Nelson's signal at Trafalgar, only there was a great deal more of it and it was raised a great deal higher.

'Here, I say, that's a bit thick,' grunted the King.

'Yes, I'm sure the Queen of Farrawania doesn't need winter knickers at this time of the year,' agreed the Queen.

'To blazes with her knickers,' growled the King. 'I mean it's a bit thick having to look at other people's washing while we're having tea. Even though it is royal washing,' he added.

'I think it's a bit ostenthingummy to have the royal arms embroidered on one's vests,' said the Queen.

'I think it's more than a bit inconsiderate to have one's washing visible from the next kingdom,' said the King.

'Right,' said the Queen. 'We shall apply to this situation the same diplomatic tact and neighbourliness we used on the occasion of the weeds over the wall and the trumpet-playing. We shall have our washing hauled up higher, and I'll see there's more of it. Go in and change all your underclothes twice.'

Within the hour the Incrediblanian washing was flying from the royal washing line higher and thicker than the Farrawanian laundry.

Next day there was more trumpeting, more foot-stamping and a salute of forty-two guns, twenty-one each for the King and Queen of Farrawania as they came haughtily into the palace of Incrediblania.

'What is it this time?' enquired the Queen of Incrediblania as sweetly as a pint of vinegar. 'Our blackbirds chirping too loudly for you? The wind rustling our leaves too much for your peace and quiet?'

The King and Queen of Farrawania sat down firmly and said even more firmly:

'It's about the washing.'

'Oh, we don't need any help with that, thank you,' said the Queen. 'We have a very adequate team of laundry ladies.'

'You've hung it up so high that we can see it from our garden,' said the Queen of Farrawania.

'And we don't like looking at other people's washing at tea-time,' said the King.

'Nor at any other time,' added the Queen.

'So kindly have it taken down at once, or preferably sooner,' they both said together.

'Certainly,' said the King of Incrediblania. 'You take down your washing so that we can't see it, then we'll do the same.'

'No,' said the Queen of Farrawania, 'I've had enough of this "you do so-and-so and we'll do the same". You take your washing down first.'

'Phooey,' said the King of Incrediblania most unmajestically.

The King and Queen of Farrawania went royal purple in the face and strode out without giving the guards a chance to present arms or stamp a single foot.

'It didn't work that time,' said the King, 'and you know I'm not sure that I like looking at our washing any more than I care about looking at theirs.'

'But if we take down our washing, we shall be able to see theirs,' protested the Queen.

'I have an idea,' said the King, scratching his head and pushing his crown crooked. 'Send for the Court Magician.'

'You remember those magic seeds and magic fertilizer you produced when we had that gardening competition,' he said to the Magician when he arrived.

'Oh, ah, yes, Majesty. Very sorry, Majesty, I had no idea it was going to be so, er . . .'

'Disastrous,' finished the King, 'but that's all over. Now's your chance to make up for it. Plant some magic tree seeds along the wall of the palace garden next to Farrawania. Water them with magic fertilizer and let's have some huge, bushy trees by tomorrow that will hide the Farrawanian washing.'

'Yes, Majesty, of course, Majesty,' gabbled the Court Magician and he went off full of determination and mumbling severe spells.

Next day down came the Incrediblanian washing and up shot the Incrediblanian trees.

But, oh, oh, that Magician had been so anxious to please

54

he'd frightfully overdone things. The trees grew so big that their bushy tops were far above the Farrawanian washing. Only the long skinny trunks hid the washing and they didn't hide it much. Hardly a stripe on the King of Farrawania's pyjamas was hidden.

'Oh dear, this is awful,' groaned the King of Incrediblania. 'Now what can we do?'

'I'll show you what we can do,' said the Queen in a voice that shrivelled two of the trees. 'Come with me.'

Outside the royal palace of Farrawania the guards stamped their feet and presented arms. Trumpet fanfares sounded. Red carpet was rolled out. Striped awnings were put up. Twenty-one gun salutes were fired.

And into the palace came the King and Queen of Incrediblania.

'Ah, how nice of you to come,' said the Queen of Farrawania.

'About time you returned our visits,' said the King.

'And what can we do for you, I hope not?' said the Queen.

The King and Queen of Incrediblania sat down and helped themselves to sugar biscuits and glasses of pale pink lemonade.

'You can take your washing down,' said the Queen of Incrediblania.

'Oh dear no, we can't,' said the Queen of Farrawania, 'not until you take down yours. That's what we said.'

'Oh dear yes, you can,' said the Queen of Incrediblania, biting off three-quarters of an emerald-green iced biscuit and making crumbs on the carpet. 'You can take your washing down because we've taken ours down, as you can see, if you care to look.'

The King and Queen of Farrawania looked at each other. They looked at the King and Queen of Incrediblania. Then they jumped up, scattering iced biscuits all over the floor and rushed out into the grounds.

'My goodness gracious, they *have* taken their washing down!' cried the King. 'Though I don't like the look of those trees.'

'Now will you be graciously pleased to do the same?' said the King of Incrediblania.

'No, we will not,' said the Queen of Farrawania. 'You don't catch us like that. The minute we take our washing down, you'll have yours up again.'

'I assure you we shall do nothing of the kind,' said the Queen of Incrediblania.

Then there was a lot of mixed-up argument about the protocol of royal washing and the priority or otherwise with which one kingdom should take down its washing before or after the aforementioned other kingdom had taken down its said washing.

'But you promised if we took our washing down, you'd do the same,' protested the Queen of Incrediblania.

'Well, the truth is,' said the Queen of Farrawania, coming over all friendly, 'our washing hides those frightful curtains in your dining-room.'

'Frightful curtains!' shrieked the Queen of Incrediblania. 'I have never heard of such a thing.'

'They're very nice curtains,' said the King of Incrediblania, who thought they were frightful himself but was going to stick up for the Queen against the common enemy.

'You get rid of those frightful curtains and we'll take down our washing,' said the Queen of Farrawania.

'Never!' cried the Queen of Incrediblania.

'Not exactly never,' said the King of Incrediblania. 'They're bound to wear out some time.'

'And then I expect you'll put up even more frightful ones,' said the Queen of Farrawania. 'That is if you can find any, which I doubt.'

The atmosphere grew extremely thick and spiky. The two Kings and the two Queens glared at each other. Was there going to be war? What! War over washing and curtains? Unthinkable.

Then something happened. It wasn't exactly what you could call a gift from Heaven, but it came from that direction. A clump of large birds who'd found the tall Incrediblanian trees just what they were looking for in the way of high-rise accommodation, accommodated themselves on the Farrawanian washing.

'Oh, my goodness!' shrieked the Queen of Farrawania.

'Oh, my pyjamas!' yelled the King of Farrawania.

They dashed into the palace. Orders were shouted, passed on, repeated, reshouted. And then down came the Farrawanian washing before the birds could start another bombing run.

'I don't think we shall have any more trouble with their washing, my dear,' said the King of Incrediblania to his wife.

'For once I agree with you, Montgomery,' said the Queen.

And, linking arms, they strolled majestically back to Incrediblania, just in time for a regal dinner, out of sight of washing of any kind but still well in sight of their own dining-room curtains, frightful or not.

6

Curtains for Count Bakwerdz

'You know,' said the Queen of Incrediblania to the King one dinner-time, 'I think Ruth was right after all.'

'Who's Ruth?' asked the King, reckoning she must be someone pretty extraordinary if the Queen thought she was right about something.

'Ruth's Queen of Farrawania next door, of course,' said the Queen, taking another helping of mauve blancmange and drowning it in cream. 'She said our dining-room curtains were frightful. Very rude of her, so of course I disagreed and put her in her place.'

'Ha,' said the King. 'I always thought it was the traditions of Farrawania that put the Queen in her place. You oughtn't to go interfering in the internal affairs of other kingdoms, you know. You'll have the United Nations after you.'

'Rubbish,' snorted the Queen. 'I'm not interested in football teams. But, after thinking things over, I think Ruth was right. These dining-room curtains are frightful. We must buy some new ones.'

'Oh,' said the King, who had rather suspected there would be something to do with buying something new to do with all this agreeing by the Queen, though he had expected it to be new dresses rather than new curtains.

'I shall see about it right away,' said the Queen, and she sent ladies-in-waiting rushing off without waiting a minute to get patterns of exotic curtain materials from the shops.

*

Choosing material for the new dining-room curtains took the Queen considerably longer than it takes most countries to choose a new government.

'I want something traditional, yet not old-fashioned,' she said. 'It must be modern and yet not advanced. I don't want anything ostentatious, but I insist upon great elegance. It mustn't be garish, but I like lots of colour and I don't want the curtains to clash with any of my dresses.'

As the Queen had more dresses than most of the shops in Incrediblania, this looked like being a bit difficult. But at last the great royal decision was made. Yards and yards of the new curtain material were ordered. And as the royal needle ladies were too busy embroidering the Queen's initials and royal arms on quantities of handkerchiefs, serviettes, pillow cases and other domestic trifles, the job of making the royal curtains was entrusted to the biggest store in Incrediblania, which put all its prices up on the strength of it.

'Now,' said the Queen, when word came that the new curtains were ready, 'have the old curtains taken down and cut up for dusters.'

'Isn't that rather a waste,' protested the King. 'They're quite good curtains. Couldn't we give them to the hospital?'

'Hospital patients don't want to be made worse by having to look at frightful curtains,' said the Queen. 'Besides,' she added, 'it wouldn't be proper for ex-royal curtains to be hung at other people's windows.'

'We could give them to the Queen of Farrawania,' suggested the King.

'Ha, ha, ha, ha,' laughed the Queen. 'Oh yes, I'd love to do that. But she'd think up something sneaky to say if I did, like "Didn't I need them for our spare bedroom to frighten off visitors?" No, they must be cut up for dusters. We need new dusters and those curtains will do just fine.' And with that, she swept out of the room.

So the frightful curtains were rolled up and given to one of the servants to carry to the Deputy Assistant Housekeeper to cut up into dusters, the Royal Housekeeper herself being a cut above jobs of that kind.

But who was that lurking outside the palace waiting for the servant with the curtains?

It was the wicked Count Bakwerdz. He'd been secretly listening to what the Queen was saying and he was planning to waylay the servant and take the curtains.

But what did Count Bakwerdz want frightful royal curtains for? Aha! He didn't want them at all. He was plotting another dire plot against the King and Queen.

'Eh, ah, um, excuse me,' he said to the servant, as he came out carrying the bundle of curtains, 'I believe those are curtains to be delivered to the Deputy Assistant Housekeeper. She has sent me to collect them. Pray allow me to take them from you.'

'Oh, yes, thank you, sir,' said the servant, who was only too glad not to have to carry the heavy bundle all the way up to the Deputy Assistant Housekeeper's attic himself. So he handed over the bundle and went back inside the palace.

'Ah, ha, my plot begins to work,' chuckled the Count. He took the curtains, but he didn't take them up to the Deputy Assistant Housekeeper at all. No, no, oh frightful dishonesty. He took them to his grim, grey castle. Not to hang at the windows, surely? Oh no, that would have let everyone see he'd stolen them. He was much too crafty for that. He hid them in a cupboard and bided his time, which is a very easy thing to do because you just do nothing and time bides itself in due course.

A little later a van drew up at the back door of the palace and Count Bakwerdz, who had been watching from his grim, grey castle with a long skinny telescope, came rushing out, jumped on a bicycle and tore up to the van just as a man got out with a large parcel. It was, as the Count suspected from the name on the van, the new dining-room curtains for the palace.

'Ah, thank you, I'll take them,' he said to the van man. He signed a squiggly squiggle on the bit of paper the van man gave him. Then as the van drove off, he hid round a corner, unwrapped the new curtains, tousled them up a bit and carried them up to the Deputy Assistant Housekeeper and gave them to her helpers.

'The Queen asked me to bring up these old curtains,' he announced. 'They are to be cut up for dusters, as I think you have been instructed.'

And off he went back to his grim, grey castle to have a good gloat.

'These curtains look very new to be cut up for dusters,' said the Deputy Assistant Housekeeper. 'I'd like them for my bedroom, but if the Queen found out she'd put me in the dungeons.'

'Yes, M'm, the Queen must be obeyed,' said one of her helpers. 'Ours not to reason why.'

'Oh, don't start reciting the "Charge of the Light Brigade",' groaned the Deputy Assistant Housekeeper. 'It's bad enough having to cut up perfectly good curtains without having to listen to poetry as well. Get out the scissors and get to work!'

So *snip, snip, slash, cut, snip,* the shears and scissors snipped and sheared away and all those lovely, gorgeous, brand new curtains were soon cut up into dusters. Very fine and gay dusters, no doubt. But oh, oh, oh, what would the Queen say when she found out?

'Now she'll have to put the old curtains back,' gloated Count Bakwerdz in his grim, grey castle across the river. 'The Queen of Farrawania will think she can't afford new ones and Incrediblania's reputation will be as much all in bits as the curtains are. Ha, ha, ha,' and he gloated a lot more.

Then he got out the old, frightful curtains, wrapped them in the paper he'd taken from the new curtains and carried the parcel to the back door of the palace, first disguising himself in a peaked cap and long coat.

'New curtains for Her Majesty,' he said, when a footman opened the door. 'Have them taken to Her Majesty at once. She's waiting for them.'

The footman took the curtains. The wicked Count went away, stuffed his disguise under a bush and crept back to look through a window and see what would happen when the Queen opened the parcel.

He was very disappointed.

No explosions occurred. The Queen's hair didn't stand on end. She didn't order anybody's head off. She didn't even stamp her foot the least little bit.

'Oh, I'm glad you've got the curtains ready. Just take them up to the Deputy Assistant Housekeeper. She knows what to do with them,' she said to the footman, thinking they were the old curtains, which, of course, they were.

So the footman took them along thinking they were the new curtains and thinking the Deputy Assistant Housekeeper had instructions to have them put up at the dining-room windows. Footmen think a lot too much sometimes.

Outside the window the wicked Count stopped gloating. He cursed, raged and then went off in the highest dudgeon he could get into.

Then suddenly he stopped, hit by an even more frightful idea than having the Queen's new curtains cut up and leaving her with the old ones. Of course, when the Deputy Assistant Housekeeper got the old curtains she wouldn't know what to do with them because she'd already cut up the other ones for dusters and she wouldn't expect two lots of curtains to cut up, would she? So, ah, ha, he'd see that she did cut up the old ones too, then the Queen would have no curtains at all for the royal dining-room.

'Ha, ha, she'll have to patch up the curtains and hang up the patchy ones in the royal dining-room. That will make Incrediblania look as shabby as shabby. Ha, ha, ha.'

And the wicked Count, gloating all over again, ran back just in time to intercept the footman, take the curtains from him and go up to the Deputy Assistant Housekeeper.

'Really,' said the Deputy Assistant Housekeeper, 'I don't know what things are coming to. Two lots of curtains to be cut up for dusters. I never heard of such a thing.'

'Oh yes you have,' snarled the Count. 'You've heard of it now, so get busy. You know what the Queen's like if her orders aren't obeyed at once, preferably a lot sooner.'

The Deputy Assistant Housekeeper shook her head, shrugged her shoulders, looked up at the ceiling and told her helpers to get on with more duster-cutting.

'It's about time those new curtains arrived,' said the Queen, looking at the bare windows of the dining-room and rather disliking them.

'I'll go along to the shop and if they're ready, I'll bring them back,' said Prince Poppup.

'Do you think you ought to?' said Princess Rosy. 'I mean it's not very princely to carry curtains, you know.'

'Oh, I don't mind, for once,' said the Prince. 'Majesty Mum's so anxious to get the new curtains up.' And off he went, but in double no time he was back in a bit of a princely dither.

'The shop says they sent the new curtains yesterday,' he said.

'Well, where are they?' asked the Queen, flinging out her hands.

'Here they are, Your Majesty,' said the Deputy Assistant Housekeeper, arriving at that moment and thinking the Queen meant the dusters. She came in followed by rows of helpers, carrying both sets of curtains neatly cut up and hemmed into the most beautiful and regal dusters.

'Here you are, Your Majesty,' she said, curtseying, 'and, though I say it myself, I think we've made those curtains into lovely dusters, though it did seem a pity.'

'What!' shrieked the Queen. 'You've cut up *both* lots of curtains? You mean to say you've cut up my lovely new curtains as well as the old frightful ones?'

'Well, er, yes, Your Majesty,' said the Deputy Assistant Housekeeper, beginning to quiver like a family-sized jelly. 'Those were Your Majesty's instructions. Count Bakwerdz himself brought them to me with your orders to cut them up.'

For a moment it looked as if the Queen was going to explode. The servants hid behind the furniture. The sun went in and the King pretended to count the roses on the wallpaper.

'Send for Count Bakwerdz!' cried the Queen, pointing a long, sharp finger at the door, and while you're about it bring the Executioner too.'

'We haven't got an Executioner, my dear,' said the King. 'You know we don't execute people. We just send them to awful places.'

The Queen stamped up and down until the rascally Count was brought in and flung on the floor with a slight bong.

'This is too much!' cried the Queen. 'You have plotted and schemed against us enough. Time after dastardly time

you have planned to seize the kingdom, or . . . or . . .'

'Do us dirt,' said the King, and he stopped counting the wallpaper roses.

'This time you have gone too far. It is . . .'

'Curtains for you,' chuckled the King, but he stopped chuckling as a long, spiky glance from the Queen hit him.

'But Your Majesty,' pleaded the Count, 'I really do not see what wrong I have done. There has been no plot. I overheard Your Majesty saying the curtains were to be cut up for dusters. I merely carried your orders to the Deputy Assistant Housekeeper.'

'You knew very well I didn't want the new curtains cut up!' cried the Queen. 'Now what sort of fitting punishment can we devise? Ah, yes,' she suddenly had an idea. Nearly as dastardly an idea as the ones the Count had. 'You will take the cut-up, old, frightful curtains and sew them together again with a blunt needle and I hope you prick your fingers,' she said. 'Then', her voice rose to a delighted screech, 'you will take them to Farrawania and give them to the Queen as a personal gift from yourself. She'll think of a much more vicious punishment for that insult than any I could imagine. Take him away!' She waved her hand and sat down.

'I wish I could see Ruth's face when she gets those frightful patched-up curtains,' she said, 'and what she'll do to that rascally Count will be something they wouldn't dare show on the telly.'

'Yes, my dear,' said the King, 'but now we haven't got any curtains for the royal dining-room.'

'Ah,' said the Queen, 'now come to think of it I wasn't really quite pleased with the material I chose for those new curtains.' She picked up one of the new dusters. 'On second thoughts I think I prefer that gold striped material we saw. We'll order new curtains made out of that. It's really rather fortunate the Count plotted as he did. And now we've got some really nice dusters as well.'

So new curtains were made and hung in the royal dining-room. The Queen of Farrawania thought they looked just as frightful as the old ones, but she had such fun giving Count Bakwerdz a right royal going over when he brought her the patched-up curtains, that she became friends with the Queen of Incrediblania once more. All was well, and the wicked Count Bakwerdz was foiled again. He'd been foiled so many times he felt like a bar of chocolate . . . very bitter chocolate.

7

Command Performance

'I rather fancy going to the theatre,' said the Queen one breakfast time. 'Let me see what's on.'

She took the newspaper away from the King, who was in the middle of failing to do the crossword, and started reading out from the theatre page.

'At the Royal Incrediblania,' she said, 'there's a musical called *Soapy Water*.'

'That sounds a bit of a wash-out,' said the King, who didn't want to go to a musical anyway and would have preferred a whodunit. He took the paper back. 'There's *Murder up the Chimney* at the Coalmarket Theatre, but that sounds like rather a smutty show.'

Princess Rosy was all for going to a nice rowdy rock concert called *Zingapuffy*, but Princess Sonia said she would prefer a quiet romantic play like *Love's Nicey Icy Creamy*, which was being performed at the Old Lavender Playhouse.

'Why don't we go to the Opera?' suggested the Queen.

'I don't like operas,' said the King, who couldn't remember having been to one, but wasn't going to take unnecessary chances. 'You can't understand the words and they always sing them in foreign languages.'

'The words don't matter,' said the Queen. 'It's the music that counts.'

'Then why don't they do away with the words and just have the music?' asked the King.

'Don't be silly,' said the Queen. 'They've got to have

words to sing. They can't just la, la it.'

Finally they decided to see a musical show at the Grand Collossus, which the King agreed to as there were plenty of dancing girls in it, hopefully with lots of legs.

'We don't want too much fuss,' said the King. 'I'll just let the manager know we're coming, so that they don't start without us in case we're late.'

So the King told the Lord Chamberlain, who told his secretary, who told the manager of the Grand Collossus theatre that Their Majesties and the Princes and Princesses would be graciously pleased to visit his theatre next Tuesday. And the manager, as soon as he'd finished banging his head on the carpet in respect, shot off and told the actors and actresses and dancing girls the great news and they all went into theatrical dithers of excitement and nearly put their eyebrows on upside down by mistake.

'I've got some shopping to do,' said the Queen to the King the next Tuesday afternoon. 'Sonia, Rosy and I will meet you and the Princes at the hat shop in the High Street at a quarter past seven. The show doesn't start until half past, so we'll have plenty of time.'

'Why don't we meet at the theatre?' said the King. 'It seems more sensible than messing about in the High Street.'

'No, no that won't do,' said the Queen. 'We don't want you waiting about outside the theatre for us, it wouldn't be regal.'

The King thought it wouldn't be very comfortable either if it happened to be raining, since the Queen was sure to be late. So he agreed they'd meet at the hat shop and went away to hope he'd enjoy the performance. He made up his mind to go to sleep during any boring love songs, but to wake up in time for the dancing girls.

The Queen and the two Princesses arrived outside the hat shop, having done their shopping and left the shops with enough things to be delivered to the royal palace to fill up more vans than the shops had.

'Look at that fur hat!' said Princess Sonia, pointing to one in the window. 'That's just the kind of hat Daddy would love to wear.'

'And it's just the kind I won't let him wear,' said the Queen. 'We don't want him going around looking like a secret agent on holiday who's about to have his cover blown.'

Princess Rosy rather fancied a somewhat dashing pale blue hat with a tall crown for Prince Poppup, and Princess Sonia would have bought Prince Egbert a cap to make him popular with the populace, but the shop was shut as it was after closing time.

'I hope Dad won't be late,' said Princess Rosy. 'It's a bit tiring standing here with everybody who passes bowing or curtseying and us having to bow back.'

'I hope the Queen isn't going to be late,' said the King to the Princes. 'Though of course she always is. Still the show won't start without us, so we needn't worry.' And he went on worrying.

They were standing outside a lady's hat shop at the other end of the High Street. But, oh dear! The Queen and the two Princesses were waiting outside a gentleman's hat shop lower down the street.

'I say, shouldn't we look comic if we wore hats like that?' said Prince Egbert, pointing to a hat that looked like a flower garden, a fruit market, an iced cake and Christmas illuminations at a carnival.

'Ha, yes,' said Prince Poppup, pointing to another hat, 'but why do ladies wear hats like that? It looks just like a man's hat.'

'There's no telling what ladies will do,' said the King.

'Good gracious, seeing that masculine-looking hat in a lady's hat shop reminds me that there's a man's hat shop at the other end of the High Street. You don't think . . .' said Prince Poppup suddenly.

'Yes, I jolly well do!' said Prince Egbert.

'You mean . . .' said the King.

'The Queen and the Princesses must be waiting at the other hat shop!' they all said at once.

'Well,' said the King, getting all organized, 'one of you had better pop up there and tell them we're here.'

So Prince Poppup popped up to the other hat shop.

But oh dear. In the meantime the Queen had remembered about the lady's hat shop at the other end of the High Street.

'I'll go down there,' said Princess Rosy, 'and tell them we're here.'

But alas and alack and other distressing noises. Princess Rosy and Prince Poppup passed each other on opposite sides of the street and didn't recognize each other as it was dark.

'If we go on like this we shall never meet,' said the King, when Princess Rosy arrived. And he sent Prince Egbert to tell the Queen and the others to meet him at the theatre.

'I meant you to meet us at the man's hat shop,' said the Queen when at last they all arrived at the theatre. 'I didn't know you knew there was a lady's hat shop in the High Street.'

'Well, when you said hat shop, I naturally thought you meant a lady's one,' said the King. 'Why did you suggest the man's hat shop?'

'Well, that's where you buy those awful hats you go shooting in,' said the Queen. 'Those ear flaps make you look like a balmy bird. I wonder people don't shoot at you when you wear it!'

Just then the manager of the theatre, who had been hopping up and down from one foot to the other, managed to get in a word.

'Oh, Most Imperial Majesties,' he gasped, bowing rapidly to everyone at once, 'I thought some important business had prevented you from coming and, as I didn't like the show to go on without you, I announced you had been

unavoidably prevented from coming and cancelled the performance.'

'You what!' cried the Queen. But just then the audience, who didn't see much point in staying if the show had been cancelled, came surging out and nearly knocked the royal party into the gutter.

'Here stop, it is my royal command that you cease!' cried the King, staggering about a bit.

'Yes,' said the two Princesses, 'we don't want to spoil your evening. Go back and we'll come in, so the show can go on.'

So the audience surged back. But the manager was still hopping up and down, as he followed the royal party to the royal box, bowing every step of the way.

'Majesties, Majesties,' he wailed. 'The show cannot go on.

When I thought Your Majesties were not coming, I sent the actors home.'

'Oh dear,' said the King, 'now what are we to do? We can't tell all these people there isn't a show after all.'

'I know,' cried Princess Rosy, Princess Sonia and the Princes, 'let's put on a show for them. It won't be as good as the real one, of course, but at least the audience will have some fun and they can have their money back anyway.'

The manager was a bit doubtful about the sort of show the Princes and Princesses could give and wasn't at all doubtful about giving the audience their money back. But the King said he would do that part.

'Now,' said Princess Sonia to the manager, 'you get the audience to sing some songs while we get ready. Then I'll do some fancy dancing for them.'

'And I'll nip back to the palace and get my magic crayons,' said Princess Rosy, 'so I can draw rows of dancing girls who'll come to life and dance too.'

So she did that. She also drew a mauve guitar for Prince Poppup. Prince Egbert did some conjuring, most of which went wrong, but it was all the funnier for that. And between them the royal Princes and Princesses kept the audience applauding and laughing until it was time to go home.

Then the King thought it was time he did a turn.

'I shall make a speech,' he said and strode on to the stage to great applause.

'Ladies and Gentlemen,' he said, 'we think it is a shame that our being delayed has deprived you of a proper professional show. So we are going to be graciously pleased to command a performance of the proper show at the palace next Monday evening. You are all invited, nothing to pay, and refreshments included.'

For that he got more applause than the real show would have got and everyone went home happy.

The Royal Command Performance was an enormous success. The actors were delighted to be taking part in it. The audience were delighted at seeing the show for nothing and getting free refreshments all at the royal palace. The Princes and Princesses were delighted that they didn't have to do a show again. The King was delighted because everyone else was delighted, and the Queen was delighted because she thought the whole thing was her idea, which it wasn't, but who was going to tell her so?

8

Answer that Door!

Ting-a-ling. Dong, dingle, dong, clang, dong, ding, dong, jangle, went the front door bell of the royal palace, because it was a highly elaborate kind of bell, something between a fire alarm, a peal of cathedral bells and the latest top pop record. The Court Magician had devised it for the Queen, who thought ordinary front door bells weren't quite regal enough for the palace.

'Ah!' said the King, who happened to be passing at the time. 'I wonder who that is?' And instead of waiting for the footman to open the door, what must he do but go and open it his royal self.

Oh dear! He shouldn't have done that. Kings aren't supposed to open front doors, never mind how fancy and elegant the front door bell may be. But His Majesty the King of Incrediblania did it. Yes, he went and opened the front door.

Immediately a person outside shoved into his arms a bundle of limp rhubarb, six large oranges, two nice hearty cabbages, two pounds of rather squashed raspberries, a curly cucumber and some straight bananas.

'Morning,' said the person. 'Thanks very much,' and off he went, slamming the palace gates with no end of a clang.

He was a very new and highly inexperienced greengrocery assistant. He'd never delivered greengroceries to a royal palace before. In fact, he had hardly ever delivered anything else anywhere else. He shouldn't have come to the front door of the palace, of course, but then the King shouldn't have opened the front door. However kings can do as they like a bit more than new and inexperienced greengrocery assistants, in spite of laws about not discriminating. And anyway the new greengrocery assistant hadn't discriminated between the front door of the palace and the back door, where he should have left the stuff.

For a moment the King stood still thinking of something to say. Then he thought of a great number of things and tried to say them all at once.

'I, ah, um, er, grrrrr, wow, pah!' he gurgled, getting his words mixed up. Rhubarb tickled his nose and made him sneeze, so he dropped some of the greengroceries. The oranges went bouncing down the High Street chased by the Royal Guards. Thank goodness there were no runner beans, or they'd never have caught them. The cabbages rolled into the Queen's rose garden, where there were already a lot of cabbage roses, so perhaps they felt at home there. The other things fell slump on to the front steps of the royal palace and the raspberries went squish all over the King's robes.

Just then an extremely fancy carriage drawn by four pink camels drew up at the palace gates and out of it came His Imperial Nobility the Nabob of Nullipop. He strode majestically up the palace steps and stopped in front of the King, who was still struggling with the greengroceries and had raspberry juice running down him.

'Ah, I make the errors,' said the Nabob to himself. 'I to the tradesmen's incoming have arrived.' He didn't recognize the King, of course, with all those greengroceries and the raspberry juice running down him. After all, you wouldn't expect a king to be covered in vegetables and raspberry juice, not even in those democratic times.

So the Nabob of Nullipop strode majestically back down the front steps and went round to the back door, thinking it must be the front door and wondering why non-Oriental countries had such queer ideas.

He rang the bell at the back door, which was an ordinary *jangle, jangle,* kind of bell because the Queen didn't want to give the servants ideas above their station. The Royal Cook opened the door, saw the Nabob and said,

'Oh, go on with ye now, Tommy. You are a one and all,

coming round here all dressed up fancy like,' and, thinking it was the greengrocer, she gave him a playful slap with a piece of pastry she had in her hands, which spread flour all over the Nabob's face.

'How dare you make the insults at me!' cried the Nabob, blowing flour off himself. 'Never have I so rude to been. First I go to a door and there are vegetables at me thrown. Now I am floured like a cake. You miserable person, fall on your face and apologize.'

'Don't you come it with me, Tommy,' said the Cook, still thinking it was the greengrocer, and she slapped some more flour on the Nabob.

The Nabob retaliated by pushing her into a basket of washing.

'That's done it!' shouted the Cook, who was a bit hot-

tempered through slaving over hot ovens. 'I'm leaving! Tell the Queen I've had enough of this place and I'm leaving,' she said to one of the maids. And she hurried off to pack her case.

Inside the palace there was slight royal confusion. The Royal Cook was packing her bags, it was nearly dinner-time and no dinner was ready.

'This is outrageous!' cried the Queen. 'How dare cooks leave. It's treason, that's what it is. Off with her head!'

'Pardon, Majesty,' said the Lord Chamberlain. 'First of all we don't know where Cook is, so we can't off her head. Secondly if we did find her and offed her head, she wouldn't be able to cook dinner, so either way it's no go.'

'Pah!' snorted the Queen, stalking into the royal kitchens. 'We shall have to get the dinner ourselves. Where's the King?'

Just then the King arrived straight from the front door, covered in vegetables and raspberry juice.

'Whatever have you been doing?' said the Queen, not really wanting to know. 'Go and put on an apron and help me get the dinner. The Cook's left.'

'Oh dear,' said the King, but he knew he'd have to do as the Queen told him, because she was that kind of queen. So he went into the kitchen, cleaned off the vegetables and raspberry juice and put on one of the Cook's aprons, which nearly covered him up.

'I'd better go and get the other vegetables the greengrocer man spilt on the front steps,' he said.

But before he could get as far as the front door the Head Footman came in and said, 'Your Majesties, His Nobility the Nabob of Nullipop has arrived.'

'Oh, my goodness!' cried the Queen, waving a saucepan and a wooden spoon. 'As if it isn't bad enough having no Cook and no dinner, here we have an Oriental visitor. Perhaps he doesn't eat dinner. Perhaps he only eats when the moon is full or something. I remember some of those Oriental monarchs who attended a Congress here a long time ago had very strange eating habits.'

The Nabob of Nullipop, who had soon come to the conclusion that the Cook wasn't the Queen, had got himself dusted down and had come back to the front door of the palace. He was picking up the vegetables (as he was a very tidy sort of Nabob) when the Head Footman had opened the door and found him.

'Quick,' said the Queen to the King in the kitchen, 'go and welcome the Nabob and keep him talking while I get the dinner ready.'

The King dashed out of the kitchen, forgetting, in his hurry, to take the Cook's apron off, tripped over it and landed in a heap at the feet of the Nabob.

'Ha!' said the Nabob. 'Some politeness at last I get. They bring the cushion.' And he sat down on the King thinking he was a cushion.

Next minute the King and the Nabob had rolled over and were in the most assorted muddle you ever saw.

Then in came the Queen, having opened tins right and left, put on kettles and given orders to the servants, so as to get some sort of dinner on the go.

'Ah, my dear Nabob, how nice of you to call!' she cried, sweeping into the drawing-room with her nose in the air and her hands outstretched.

Then she stopped with a gasp. There was no Nabob there. Neither was there any sign of the King.

'I can't understand it,' she murmured. 'Surely the Nabob can't have rung the bell and run away? No, no, perhaps the King has taken him for a walk. Very clever of him. Give me time to get the dinner arranged.' She sat down on a couch, which immediately shot her off because the King and the Nabob had rolled under it in their struggles, and when the Queen sat on it they felt a bit squashed down.

Her Majesty gave the couch one of her Do-as-I-tell-you looks and it began to crawl across the room because the King and the Nabob wanted to get out from under it.

'Help!' cried the Queen.

'Help!' cried the King, but as he was under the couch nobody heard him.

The Nabob couldn't shout anything. He had his mouth full of carpet.

The couch crept back nearer and nearer the Queen. She jumped on to a very expensive table. The couch started pushing the table round the room with the Queen dancing up and down on it, using steps she didn't know she could do.

The door flew open. Guards burst in. They saw what was happening, didn't believe it and burst out again, as they didn't want to get involved with queens being chased round the room by couches.

Round and round went the couch with the King and the Nabob under it. Round and round went the Queen trying to get away from it.

Suddenly the King's apron got caught in the legs of the couch and tore itself free. The couch ran into a wall and tipped over. The King and the Nabob struggled to their feet. The Queen, sprawled in the most unmajestic fashion on the carpet, got up as well and they all three looked at each other, not believing anything.

The Nabob found his tongue first and was just about to use it to declare war when a herald came rushing in, tripped over the couch, got up, bowed and fell over again, stood up once more and blurted out in frantic tones to the Nabob,

'Your Imperial Nobility,' he gasped, 'word has just reached us that the nearby kingdom of Snatchitania has invaded Nullipop.'

'Good gracious!' cried the King and Queen, and the Nabob said much the same thing only ten times worse in his own language. The Queen forgot to ask what the King and the Nabob were doing under the couch. And they forgot to explain why they were there and anyway they weren't too sure.

'I must leave at once!' cried the Nabob. 'My kingdom must be defended.'

'I think', said the King, 'we owe it to Your Imperial Nobility to help you defeat the enemy. After all that business with vegetables at the front door and runaway couches, it is the least we can do.'

'Of course,' said the Queen.

The King gave orders for the Army and Navy to be mobilized to leave at once for the kingdom of Nullipop. But oh, dismal disaster! Most of the Army were on holiday, some of the others were ill in bed and the rest didn't look too keen about having to fight someone else's war.

Princess Rosy hurriedly drew a lot of soldiers with her magic crayons. But she was in such a scribbling panic to get them done, they didn't look as if they could fight much. Fortunately they all blew away before they could pop up properly alive.

'Alas, I must go it alone!' cried the Nabob.

But ha! What were those specks in the sky? Were they

Snatchitanian aircraft coming to bomb Incrediblania? No, they couldn't be. Aeroplanes didn't exist there yet. No, good gracious! As the specks drew nearer and became larger they turned out to be the three vegetarian dragons who had got fed up with Count Bakwerdz's cooking and left the kingdom. They landed in clouds of coloured smoke at the feet of the King and the Nabob.

'We heard,' panted dragon one, 'that your kingdom is being attacked and we also heard you were here,' said dragon two, 'so we came to help,' said dragon three. 'Between us we will help you defeat the enemy.'

'Hurray!' cried the Nabob.

'However did you hear about all that?' asked the Queen, who was keenly interested in ways of hearing about things, as she liked a bit of gossip.

'We heard it on the antirrhinums—the snapdragons, you know,' said the dragons. 'It's the dragon version of the grape vine. They're flowers with little mouths that tell us things.'

'Splendid!' cried the King. 'My good dragons, how nice of you to help.'

So off went the Nabob, the King and what was available of the King's Army, with the dragons flying ahead.

Soon they arrived in Nullipop and there, sure enough, the Nabob's troops were engaged fighting the Snatchitanians.

The three dragons flew over the enemy in formation. They peeled off one by one and dived on the Snatchitanians, belching fire of the best quality.

Zoom, sizzle, roar! Ziziziziziziz, boom!

That did it. The Snatchitanian Army wasn't equipped with anti-dragon artillery and wouldn't have had time to use it if it had. In almost no time at all it was routed, put to flight, beaten, driven off, defeated and generally made to wish it hadn't come. And His Severe Sinisterness the High Grabber of Snatchitania ran away and got into trouble with his wife for being late for tea.

'How can I thank you?' cried the Nabob of Nullipop afterwards to the King of Incrediblania. 'Thanks to your good dragon friends, my kingdom is saved.'

'Good old dragons!' said Princess Sonia and Princess Rosy, who had come, with their husbands, along with the King and Queen and the Army.

'I shall find a nice quiet corner of Nullipop for them to stay as long as they like,' said the Nabob. 'But now I must think of a suitable reward for Your Majesty. But come, let us have dinner while I think.'

'Good,' said the Queen, who always thought she could think better after a good dinner.

So they all went into the Nabob's palace for a good nosh-up and think.

And if you want to know what the Nabob thought up, you'll have to read the next story.

9

The Royal Reward

'You have saved my kingdom,' said the Nabob of Nullipop, popping a lollipop into his mouth as he and the King and Queen of Incrediblania and the Princesses and Princes sat talking after dinner. 'You have driven off the invaders of Nullipop and all is peace. I must reward you suitably.'

'Oh, no, not at all,' said the King. 'It was the least we could do.'

'Ah, but your least it was the most,' said the Nabob. 'Now let me think of a suitable reward.' He glanced round the table and saw the two Princesses, who were certainly well worth seeing.

'Aha! I have it,' he cried, clapping his hands, which caused fifty-seven assorted servants to come rushing in and bang their foreheads on the floor. 'I shall present you with gold to the combined weights of your so charming daughters.'

'Good gracious!' exclaimed the King, and the Queen nearly fainted at the thought of so much money, but managed to stay unfainted so as to hear what came next.

'We shall weigh the two Princesses,' said the Nabob, 'and gold to their combined weight shall be presented to Incrediblania for saving the kingdom of Nullipop.'

'Oh dear,' thought Princess Sonia, 'I wish I hadn't done all that slimming. This is one occasion when it pays to be fat.'

'I've heard of people being worth their weight in gold,' said Princess Rosy, 'but I never thought it could be me.'

'Come then,' said the Nabob, getting up, 'we shall arrange

the royal weighing to take place in the courtyard tomorrow.'

But oh dear! All during this conversation someone was lurking outside listening. It was the wicked Count Bakwerdz. He'd come to Nullipop with the King on the pretext that he wished to lead his regiment into action against the Snatchitanians. It was a nice brave thing to say because he didn't have a regiment. But the King couldn't very well say he couldn't come and, anyway, if he'd left him behind in Incrediblania, he'd have tried to seize the throne in the King's absence. So here he was, lurking outside the banqueting hall. And not only lurking, but plotting. 'People being given their weight in gold,' he muttered. 'That gives me an idea.' It certainly did. A dastardly idea.

'I can't wangle it so as to get weighed for my weight in gold,' he said to himself, 'but I have another idea. This will make the Nabob change his mind about being grateful to the King. This will cause him to declare war on Incrediblania. Then I shall seize the throne and be King myself, ha, ha, ha, ha.' He gloated so much he gave himself tummyache, headache, toothache and spots before the eyes. But he reckoned it was worth it.

Next day the courtyard of Nullipop was arranged for the grand royal weighing ceremony. The scales were set up with a platform big enough for the two Princesses to stand on and a big basket on the other side to take the gold, which was piled up in bags nearby. The two Princesses wore their weightiest make-up and ate good hearty breakfasts, partly because they were hungry and partly in the hope of making themselves a few gold pieces heavier.

'Let the weighing commence,' commanded the Nabob.

The two Princesses stepped daintily on to the scales.

Attendants picked up bags of gold and placed them carefully on the other side.

The scales didn't move. The Princesses' side stayed firmly down.

'More gold!' cried the Nabob, and the attendants put more bags on the scales.

Still the scales didn't move.

'You haven't got any lead weights stuffed up your jersey, have you?' whispered Princess Rosy to Princess Sonia. 'You know, like jockeys have to have so that the horses can't run too fast.'

'Of course not,' whispered Princess Sonia. 'It must be those three extra sausages I had for breakfast.'

'More gold!' cried the Nabob, not quite so loudly this time.

Another bag or two of gold was put on the scales, but there was still no movement.

'Our daughters can't be as heavy as all that,' said the Queen.

'Shush,' said the King out of the side of his mouth, 'let's be thankful for nice heavy daughters, if they bring the gold in.'

'More gold,' squeaked the Nabob, beginning to turn slightly pale yellowy green.

On went more bags of gold, but still the scales didn't move. The attendants put on all the bags of gold they had and still the Princesses seemed to be heavier, which they couldn't have been.

'Send for more gold,' gasped the Nabob, his ears beginning to droop.

But even with still more gold on the scales they didn't move.

'I can't understand it,' murmured the King.

'I'm not sure this isn't a bit insulting,' said Princess Sonia. 'I reckon their rotten old scales don't work properly.'

'Belt up,' whispered Princess Rosy. 'It means more gold for Dad and that means bigger birthday presents for us.'

'This understand I cannot,' groaned the Nabob. 'How is it that such slim and dainty girls can weigh so terrifically much?'

Just then there was a slight puff of technicolour smoke and an enormous and very fancy elephant appeared behind the two Princesses. His front feet had been weighing down their side of the scales all the time! What dastardly cheating was this!

There was an uproar. Shouts went up. Growls took place. The Nabob went thirty different colours, all of them unpleasant.

'So,' he yelled, 'it is the cheatings you do! This is how you take the advantages of me. Because you save my kingdom, you now try to cheat me out of all my gold. Now there shall be war again and it shall be against Incrediblania!'

'But it's nothing to do with us!' cried the King. 'I know nothing about elephants, invisible or otherwise. I don't understand it.'

'Oh yes, he does,' shouted a nasty voice, and the wicked Count Bakwerdz came running up, leering and sneering and gloating all at once.

He pointed a long skinny finger at the King. 'He told his Court Magician to make one of your elephants invisible,' he cried, 'and then he had it brought here to stand on the scales and make it seem as if the Princesses were heavier than all your gold.'

'Miscreant!' yelled the Nabob to the King. 'Evil-doer,

swindler, cheater, trickster, bamboozler, diddler, fiddler, villain . . .'

'No, no, no, no,' cried the King, before the Nabob could think up any more insulting names to call him, 'I am none of these; I am innocent of all these charges.'

'Pah!' snorted the Nabob. 'That is one of my favourite elephants. I recognize him. Fetch your Court Magician whom you instructed to make him unseeable.'

'Oh, I don't think that is necessary,' said the Count in an oily, melted margarine sort of voice, 'the evidence is clear. Or at least it is now that the elephant has become visible. You didn't expect that did you?' he swung round at the King. 'You thought you were going to get away with it. But I guessed your nasty plot. I told the Court Magician to remove the spell because you were cheating His Imperial Nobility.'

'This is a plot!' cried the King to the Nabob. 'But it is this person, the wicked Count Bakwerdz, who has plotted it. He is always plotting against me. I only brought him here because he would have plotted to seize my throne if I had left him at home.'

'Pah! What an excuse!' exclaimed the wicked Count.

'I shall settle this!' cried the Nabob. 'Let the Court Magician of Incrediblania be brought before us.'

The Court Magician, who had come to Nullipop with the King of Incrediblania, took a bit of finding because he'd made himself invisible, as he was rather wont to do. But at last Prince Egbert found him by the very practical method of falling over him, as he hadn't been able to see him. Then the Magician thought he'd better become visible so as to apologize for causing the Prince to fall over, because, as the history books tell you, the fall of princes can be a very serious matter.

But this wasn't very serious because Prince Egbert laughed and thought it was rather a joke. 'Ha, ha,' he said, 'I found you because I couldn't find you, that's why I fell over you.

Now come along, the King wants you. There's some trouble about invisible elephants.'

'Oh, that's all right, Your Highness,' said the Magician, arranging his robes carefully, 'I know all about that.'

'Ooer!' thought the Prince. 'That means the King really did plot against the Nabob as Count Bakwerdz said, but I still don't believe it.'

As soon as they arrived before the Nabob, the Court Magician made an elaborate bow, produced a rather bent orange and changed it into the flag of Nullipop, which he waved majestically.

'I trust Your Imperial Nobility is pleased with the magical surprise Count Bakwerdz instructed me to arrange for you,' he said. 'The sudden appearance of your elephant from nowhere was I feel sure a most entertaining event.'

'Gr-r-r-r!' snarled Count Bakwerdz, seeing his plot come apart in mid air.

'What is that you are saying?' said the Nabob. 'You tell me Count Bakwerdz told you to make my elephant disappear and then make him stand on the scales to cheat me of my gold?'

'No, no, no, Your Imperial Nobility,' gabbled the Court Magician. 'The Count told me to make one of your elephants disappear and then make it reappear in the middle of some ceremony Your Imperial Nobility was to conduct. I know nothing about gold and I certainly would not wish to cheat you.'

'There, I told you so!' said the King. 'Count Bakwerdz at his old games again. What am I to do with the fellow? If I'd left him at home he'd have plotted to steal the throne in my absence. So I bring him with me and he plots to involve me in wars with our friend the Nabob.'

'Ah, ha!' said the Nabob. 'If it is a question of not knowing what to do with this villain,' he pointed at the Count, who shrunk back against the elephant, which picked him up in its trunk and plonked him back down at the feet of the Nabob. 'If that is the question,' continued the Nabob, sounding a bit like Shakespeare, which was clever of him as he didn't know who Shakespeare was, 'I can soon settle that. I will sentence this rascally Count, who is so fond of messing about with my elephants, to be trodden on by ten elephants. That will stop his plotting, ha, ha, yes!'

'No, no, no!' cried the King. 'Although the Count is a villain, a miscreant and all those other things you called me by mistake, we don't take revenge on people like him in Incrediblania. We must think of a just punishment, but nothing dangerous.'

'Very well,' said the Nabob, 'I have the nice idea. An elephant it shall still be. I have a very nice pale blue one which requires constant washing. The Count shall stay here and wash my blue elephant every day as punishment for plotting against you.'

'Well,' said the Queen, who hadn't spoken for so long the King thought she must have gone to sleep, 'I think that takes care of that nasty Count very nicely.'

'Yes, yes,' said the King, 'I think washing a pale blue elephant every day will keep him out of mischief.'

'Agreed,' cried the Nabob. He clapped his hands and the Count was led away to start his elephant-washing.

'But now,' said the King, 'we cannot possibly accept all this gold. Count Bakwerdz plotted to make it look as if we were cheating you. We weren't, of course, but I don't think we can accept any gold now.'

'Oh, I don't know,' said the Queen, who hardly ever

admitted to not knowing anything. 'It would come in handy.'

'Of course, of course,' said the Nabob, 'we shall weigh the Princesses again, this time without any elephants and you shall have their weight in gold, as I promised, for saving my kingdom.'

'Oh well, if you say so,' said the King.

So everything ended happily. The wicked Count Bakwerdz was out of the way for a bit and the kingdom of Incrediblania was as rich as a Christmas pudding made with a thousand eggs, marzipan covering and chocolate icing.

10

Scampering Scarecrows

His Majesty the King of Incrediblania was acting in a most unmajestic manner. He was dancing up and down waving his hands. He was shouting very unroyal things.

'Shooh!' he shouted. 'Go away! Scram! Be off!'

A clump of assorted birds rose into the air like an astonished jump-jet. They hovered for a bit until the King got out of breath and stopped shouting and dancing about, then they came down again and went on eating the royal fruit on the royal fruit trees and bushes.

'Go away!' screeched the King. 'It is my royal command that you fly off and leave our fruit alone.'

The birds obediently rose up in a clump once more, but came down again the moment the King stopped shouting.

Louder and louder shouted the King. He rushed up and down the garden waving his arms. His robes flew out and waved in the wind, so that he looked rather like an improbable bird himself.

'Shoo-, most frightfully, -oo!' he yelled. Then feeling too exhausted to shout any more, he went in to tea.

And the moment he got inside, the birds came back.

'Something will, puff, puff, have to be, puff, done about those, puff, birds,' he said, sitting down and taking a piece of cake without having bread and butter first, which you aren't supposed to do, but kings can do as they like as long as queens will let them.

'Why don't you get a scarecrow?' said the Queen, pouring

out tea and moving the cake away from the King, who was
still too out of breath to eat the piece he'd taken.

'A, who, ho?' gasped the King.

'A scarecrow,' said the Queen. 'You know, one of those
frightening-looking figures dressed in old clothes.'

'You don't mean Aunt Jane,' said the King, hoping the
Queen wasn't going to ask her to come and scare the birds,
because she always rather scared him, being a bit on the
fierce side as she was.

'No, no, no,' said the Queen, 'I mean one of those things

you put in a field or garden to scare the birds away. A scarecrow.'

'I don't think we get many crows,' said the King. 'They're mostly sparrows and starlings. Perhaps we need a scare-sparrow or a frightstarling.'

'Well, whatever you call it,' said the Queen, 'that's the sort of thing we need, so you'd better get one before those wretched birds scoff up all my raspberries, blackberries and currants and peck holes in my favourite apples. I can't see,' she went on, 'why a bird can't just eat an apple like any reasonable human being, instead of taking a peck out of every one on the tree. Their mothers don't bring them up properly, that's what it is.'

'I hope you aren't going to suggest we have mother-care classes for birds,' said the King. 'But, yes, I think it's a good idea to have a scare-what's-its-name to frighten the birds off our fruit. I'll get the ministers to make one. There isn't much ruling to do in this hot weather, so they might as well make us a . . .'

'Scarecrow,' said the Queen. 'Yes, a good idea. It will keep them out of mischief.'

The King tried hard to imagine the Lord Chief Justice getting into mischief by not making a scarecrow, but didn't succeed.

'Now,' said the King, when he'd gathered all the ministers and court officials together, 'I want a really alarming scarecrow. Pull out all stops and pull no punches. Let it be a hundred and five per cent terrifying thing that no bird will dare to come within miles of. And don't be too long making it, or the summer will be over and there'll be no fruit left to protect and no birds to scare away.'

'Yes, Majesty, of course, Majesty, at once, Majesty,' gabbled some of the ministers, but others seemed rather more reluctant.

'I don't really care for splishing about with paint and old clothes if that's what it means,' said the Lord High Admiral. 'I have plenty of sailors who could do the job. They can splice ropes and scrub decks and all that nautical stuff, so they'd think nothing of making a scarecrow.'

'I don't think much of that,' said the King. 'We can't have the Navy occupied making a scarecrow and leave the kingdom undefended. Suppose there was an invasion?'

'Ha, yes,' said the Lord High General, 'I was going to suggest my men could do the job, though they've really enough to do spitting and polishing all over the place. But as you say, defending the nation against enemies is more important than defending the royal fruit against birds.'

'I didn't say that,' said the King. 'Anyway, there isn't any invasion or war and I can do any ruling that's needed . . .'

'With my help,' said the Queen in a rather snap and crackle voice. 'Now,' she went on, 'you all get some old clothes and paint and cardboard and stuff, and set about making a scarecrow to scare all scarecrows.'

And with that she swept out, followed by the King.

In one of the larger sheds in the royal gardens the ministers were busy making the scarecrow.

'You'll have to do it out in the shed,' the Queen had ordered. 'I don't want you making a mess with paint and glue and stuff on my best carpets.'

So inside the shed the ministers were hard at it making a mess with paint and glue and stuff, not on the Queen's best carpets, because even the best sheds in the royal gardens didn't have carpets. Even the Queen thought that would be a bit too ostenthingummy.

'We must make this scarecrow really terrifying,' said the Lord Chamberlain, sloshing away with paint on a cardboard box. He painted a frightful face, chiefly because it was the only kind of face he could paint. He used pink and green and purple paint, and plenty of it.

'It's a good job we put our old clothes on for this job,' said the Lord Chancellor. 'The Queen wouldn't half have gone on if we'd got paint on our best robes.'

'A bit unfair I call it,' said the Lord High Keeper of Coalscuttles, who was apt to get coal smudges on his best robes.

'Not half!' agreed the Minister of Agriculture, daubing paint on an old coat. He swung his paint brush a bit wide and sloshed a dollop of green paint across the face of the Minister of Education.

'Pwouff!' said the Minister in a very educated voice. He tried to rub the paint off his face and got some in his eyes. Luckily it was harmless water paint so didn't hurt, but he couldn't see properly for all the gooey mess.

'Give me a towel or a rag or something!' he cried. He waddled across the room, tripped over a pile of old clothes and fell head first into the cardboard box on which the Lord Chamberlain had painted that frightful face.

'Look out!' cried the Lord Chamberlain.

But the Minister of Education couldn't look out. His head was stuck fast in the box. He started running round the room, knocking into the others and getting paint of all colours on his clothes which, thank goodness, were his old ones.

He staggered about waving his hands, trying to find his

way. Then he came to the open door and staggered out into the royal gardens.

Up a tree nearby sat a fairy, doing some fairy knitting.

'Oh dear!' she said, when she saw the Minister of Education with the frightful box on his head. 'Whatever are they up to now? It reminds me of the time they had to make a dummy king in Astufflavia, to take the real King's place at a conference and I brought it to life, not knowing it was going to cause trouble.'*

She knitted a few stitches and went on, to herself as there were no other fairies up the tree to talk to, 'I'm going to keep out of this. No spells to bring anything to life or try to put things right. I shall just mind my own business this time.' And she went on minding it and doing her knitting at the same time which is easy enough, if you know how to do it.

Down below all was in uproar. The Minister of Education with paint all over his old clothes and his head stuck fast in the box with the frightful face painted on it was half way through the royal rose garden.

'We must stop him before the Queen sees him,' said the Lord Chamberlain, 'or Her Majesty will be as wild as wild at one of us going about in that state. She'll wonder what the neighbours will think.'

'I think it's silly to do that,' said the Lord Chancellor. 'What's the use of worrying about what the neighbours will think? They're probably worrying about what you'll think, so if nobody thought, nobody need worry.'

'Stop talking and get after him!' cried the Lord Chamberlain, cramming on an old hat, which had been intended for

* See 'The King with the Paper Face' in *The Dribblesome Teapots*.

the scarecrow in case he caught cold as his hair was a bit on the scarce side. 'Come on, we must catch him before the Queen sees him.'

So out of the shed and across the royal gardens went the ministers in their old clothes with paint of all colours on their faces and unlikely hats on their heads.

'There he goes!' cried the Lord Chancellor, pointing without remembering to put his paint brush down, so the Lord Chamberlain got a slosh of purple paint down one cheek.

Across the royal rose garden and over the royal lawns went the ministers making the most frightful sight the garden had ever seen.

'I'll go along and see how the ministers are getting on with the scarecrow,' said the Queen, 'and, if they've been idling their time, I shall know just what to say to them.'

She walked majestically across the lawn. Then she suddenly stopped and let out an exceedingly unmajestic screech.

'Owwwwwww!' she cried.

For coming towards her, blundering from side to side was a most terrifying figure with a square head and a fearsome face and all dressed in ragged clothes.

Of course it was the Minister of Education still trying to get the box off his head and still trying to find out where he was going. But the Queen thought it was the scarecrow that the ministers were making, come to life.

'Oh, my goodness!' she cried. 'This is awful!' She turned and ran back to the palace.

'Help!' she cried. 'The scarecrow has come to life! Fetch the guards!'

'I don't believe it,' said the King. He ran out into the

grounds and found he not only believed it, he believed it several times over. For rushing about the lawn was the Minister of Education, still with his head in the box, being followed round by the other ministers. And what with having their old clothes on and what with having splashes of paint on their clothes and on their faces, and some with unlikely hats on their heads and some with tangled hair with bits of cardboard stuck on, they all looked like scarecrows. And they were all very much alive.

'Help!' shouted the King.

Then down from the tree flew the fairy, her knitting in one hand and her fairy wand in the other.

'Who are you?' demanded the King. 'Go away. We're having enough trouble with scarecrows coming to life without Christmas tree fairies littering the place up.'

'I'm not a Christmas tree fairy, I'm a real one,' said the fairy.

'Now, now, now,' said a voice, and the Queen arrived with some guards. 'Who is this person and doesn't she know you can't knit with a knitting-needle a yard long with a star on one end?'

'That's my fairy wand,' said the fairy, 'and I'm a fairy.'

By this time the minister scarecrows had caught up with the Minister of Education, who came running back towards the King and Queen, holding out his arms to help him find his way about.

'This is your doing!' cried the Queen, pointing to the fairy, while the guards hurriedly took cover under ornamental bushes in proper military style when faced by an enemy. 'You've brought these scarecrows to life. Now kindly turn them back into proper scarecrows and let's have no more of your nonsense.'

The fairy put down her knitting on the grass, where it was seized by the palace cat, who ran off with it.

'I beg your pardon, Your Majesty,' she said, 'but all this is nothing to do with me. I have not brought any scarecrows to life. Why should I? Nobody wants live scarecrows scampering about the place. They're supposed to stand still like this and scare birds.'

She stretched out her arms and scared the King by bringing the star on her wand rather near his nose.

'I don't care what you have or have not done,' said the Queen. 'Kindly turn these things back into lifeless scarecrows at once!'

Oh, dreadful situation! The Queen didn't know the scarecrows were really her ministers. If the fairy magicked them into scarecrows there'd be no ministers left to attend to affairs of state, which would be a fine state of affairs. And the poor ministers would be left standing about scaring away birds, which is no sort of work for a Minister of the Crown.

'Turn those scampering things into scarecrows and do it now, instantly!' commanded the Queen again.

The fairy shrugged her shoulders.

'Well,' she said, 'if that's what you want, but don't blame me for anything.'

She raised her wand, just as the Minister of Education broke away from the other ministers and came trundling up to the Queen. The fairy's wand knocked the painted box off his head and he stood there goggling.

'Good gracious!' exclaimed the Queen. 'If it isn't the Minister of Education!'

'Well if it isn't him, who jolly well is it?' said the King, peering at the Minister of Education. 'He looks a bit the worse for wear but I recognize him all right. What's he got up like a scarecrow for?'

'P-pup-please, Your Majesty,' spluttered the Minister of Education, 'we were making a scarecrow, as Your Majesty instructed us, and I got this box stuck on my head.'

'And we tried to catch him before he scared anybody,' said the other ministers, rushing up, all looking more like scarecrows than real scarecrows do, with their old clothes and splodges of paint all over them and some with unlikely hats on their heads.

'Do you want me to turn these gentlemen into scarecrows or don't you?' asked the fairy, getting a bit impatient because it was getting near time for her nectar-break.

'Oh no, for goodness' sake, don't,' cried the Queen, waving her hands. 'We thought they were scarecrows come to life. For goodness' sake don't make them into real scarecrows or we'll have nobody to do any ruling.'

'No,' said the King, 'that would be most awkward. There'd be nobody to minister the agriculture and fisheries, which would mean no cabbages and a shortage of fish and chips. There wouldn't be anyone to minister to education and we'd all have to go metric so as to be able to add up. And, worst of all, there wouldn't be anybody to chancel the exchequer and that would mean we shouldn't get any taxes in to pay for the Queen's new dresses.'

'Oh dear, yes!' cried the Queen very faintly, going as pale as a sheet just washed in biological washing powder. 'But it's all right. Now go and fetch the scarecrow, so that we can keep the birds off the royal fruit, which was all that we wanted in the first place.'

'Alas, Your Majesty,' said the Minister of Agriculture, 'we didn't get time to finish the scarecrow. Shall we go and finish it now?'

'No,' said the King, 'for goodness' sake don't let's have any more nonsense with scampering scarecrows!'

'But how are we going to keep the birds off the fruit?' asked the Queen, beginning to see visions of no apple pies, a complete absence of blackcurrant jam and not a single raspberry jelly.

'I think I can help,' said the fairy. 'I'll have a word with the birds and ask them to keep off your fruit.'

So off she flew, and she must have had a very persuasive way of chatting up birds, because after that there was never so much as a nibble on an apple or a peck at the raspberries.

11

The Court Fuddelfey

Breakfast in the royal palace of Incrediblania was raging quite peacefully. The Queen was stopping the King from having enough sugar on his porridge. The two Princesses were eating half nothing in case it made them fat. Prince Poppup was on his second egg, and Prince Egbert was attacking a kipper with great bravery and the wrong knife and fork.

Then right in the middle of this happy domestic scene something happened.

The King had an idea.

When the chandeliers had stopped swaying. After the Queen had nearly swallowed her spoon as well as her porridge. When Prince Poppup had scooped his second egg off the carpet and the two Princesses had eaten a whole cornflake each, they were so astonished, the King spoke. In a voice that sounded like the best marmalade, he said:

'I think we should have a Court Fairy.'

'A what!' gulped the Queen, spattering porridge down her robes.

The two Princesses clapped their hands over their mouths in the most unroyal manner, and Prince Egbert let his kipper escape.

'Well,' said the King, taking some toast, 'you know that fairy person who saved the ministers from being turned into scarecrows. Well I think we should make her Court Fairy, so that she can do a bit of magic for us when we need it.'

'But', said the Queen, 'she didn't do any magic. She just refrained from doing it. Anyway, we already have a Court Magician.'

'Oh, him,' said the King in a voice that scorched the edges of his toast. 'What use is he? Those awful disappearing eggs.'

'And his colour-changing handkerchiefs always get stuck in the middle,' said Prince Poppup.

'Oh, I think he's rather sweet,' said Princess Sonia, 'and he can do some real magic now and then. Look at that invisible elephant.'

'You can't look at invisible elephants,' said the King, 'and anyway that was awful. He nearly got himself involved in a plot with that dreadful Count Bakwerdz.'

'It might provide a little competition,' said the King, who rather fancied the idea of having an attractive fairy around the place.

So the appointment of a Court Fairy was agreed, but the fairy herself seemed a bit doubtful.

'Of course, I'm ever so pleased you want me as Court Fairy,' she said, 'but I ought to tell you I'm a bit of a fuddelfey. I mean I'm not awfully certain about my magic. I must tell you this, otherwise I'd be offending against the Trade Descriptions Act, whatever that is, and I don't want the Amalgamated Union of Fairies, Witches, Warlocks, Magicians, Prestidigitators, Enchanters and Bogey Men coming down on me.'

'You mean you might turn the King into a frog while trying to conjure up a magnificent banquet?' asked the Queen, looking sideways at the King and wondering whether he'd be easier to boss about if he were a frog. But then she decided she wouldn't want him hopping about all over the place and getting in the way of the housekeeping.

'Oh, no, Your Majesty,' protested the fairy, 'nothing so drastic as that! I'd be very careful about anything on a grand scale of course.'

So that made the King feel safe from being turned into a frog by mistake and the fairy was installed as Court Fairy.

But the Queen was still seized by frightful doubts about the idea.

Two and one fifth days later, frenzied screams came shrieking from the Queen's boudoir.

'My diamonds!' she cried. 'They've been stolen, purloined, grabbed, pilfered, burgled, pinched, filched! Fetch the police, no, no, no, don't fetch the police, fetch the Court Fairy. Oh, oh, oh, oh.'

She came rushing down the stairs three at a time, causing such a draught that the pictures of the King's ancestors went crooked, including one that already looked rather crooked as it had been painted by a very advanced artist.

Pandemonium began to reign, which is something only the King and Queen are supposed to do. Servants ran about. The Court Magician hurriedly vanished a cup of coffee and a bun, and came tearing in.

'Where's the Court Fairy?' cried the Queen. 'Tell her to come here at once and get my diamonds back!'

'Here I am, Your Majesty,' said the fairy, suddenly appearing in a puff of rather second-hand smoke from behind an even more second-hand antique vase. 'What is Your Majesty's wish?'

'Never mind wishes!' cried the Queen. 'My diamond necklace has gone. Find out who took it and where it is. Get it back, arrest the criminal and turn him into something harmless, but unpleasant.'

At the back of the room Princess Sonia whispered something to Princess Rosy. 'It seems rather a coincithingummy,' she said.

'Dence,' said Princess Rosy.

'No, I'm not!' said Princess Sonia.

'Coinci-dence,' said Rosy. 'I was only finishing your word for you, since I never get a chance to finish your chocolates.'

'Never mind,' said Princess Sonia, 'but I think it's a bit odd that Mum should lose her diamond necklace almost the very moment the fairy is made Court Fairy.'

'Ooh, yes,' said Princess Rosy. 'I wonder if she's just pretending to have lost it to test the fairy.'

'We may never know,' groaned Princess Sonia, who couldn't bear not to know things, and then she turned her attention back to the matter in hand.

The fairy looked up at a chandelier on the ceiling of the great hall, noticed that it had a cobweb on it, did a spell to abolish the cobweb and abolished a quarter of the chandelier by mistake. She tried another spell to restore the chandelier and produced ten more cobwebs. Then she gave up and gave her undivided attention to the dire question of the Queen's missing diamond necklace.

She took a fairy look between layers of air.

'Aha!' she cried. 'I know where the diamond necklace is.'

'Where is it?' cried the Queen, panting like a horse that has just run the Grand National in ten minutes.

'Ssh,' murmured the fairy, 'I must have absolute quiet while I make a magic spell to bring back the missing jewels.'

Silence reigned instead of pandemonium. The King and Queen were being done out of a lot of reigning that day.

The fairy shut her eyes. She waved her wand. She muttered a spell.

For a moment nothing happened. Then there was a slight whistling sound. A little whisp of smoke appeared on the table, spun round and turned into something.

'Is that the Queen's diamond necklace?' said the fairy, opening her eyes.

It was a page of last year's calendar with a tea stain on it.

'Pah!' snorted the Queen. 'If that's the best you can do I don't think much of it. I could do better myself. In fact,' she said with a funny look in her eyes, 'I shall do better myself. I shall find out where the missing necklace is.' And she stamped regally upstairs, kicking up rather a dust.

Princess Sonia started whispering to Princess Rosy again.

'There you are,' she whispered, 'I'm sure Mum didn't really lose her necklace at all. She just hid it to test the Court Fairy. Now she'll bring it triumphantly down and say the fairy's no good.'

She'd hardly whispered the last whisp, when frenzied screams came from the Queen's boudoir for the second time that day. Only this time they were much more frenzied.

'Fetch the police! Turn out the Guard!' yelled the Queen, coming downstairs four at a time. 'My diamonds! My diamonds!'

'Didn't you succeed in finding them after all, Your Majesty?' asked the fairy in a voice so sweet it took your appetite away.

Oh dear! Things were getting a bit awful. The Queen had hidden her diamonds, just as Princess Sonia had guessed. She put them in an old shoe-box and pretended they were lost, so as to test the fairy and see if she really could do magic. But when she went to get them the shoe-box was empty. Not a diamond in sight. A complete absence of jewels. Now they really were lost. Ooer.

'Don't just stand there!' screamed the Queen, as everyone hung around with their mouths opening and shutting in surprise till they looked like a tribe of unlikely goldfish. 'My diamonds have gone. Search the grounds! Search the vaults! Bring out the Military! Sound the fire alarm! Do something! My diamonds must be found!' Then she caught sight of the fairy, who was wearing a very smug sort of expression. And if you've never seen a fairy looking smug, you've missed one of the seven sights of storyland.

'You . . .' cried the Queen, going several very unsuitable colours. 'I believe *you* stole my diamonds. Yes, you stole them so that you could pretend to discover them with your magic. Pah! You're nothing more than a, than a . . .' She couldn't think what the fairy was no more than, so she cried, 'Guards arrest her! She has stolen my diamonds! Fling her into the dungeons!'

The guards rushed at the fairy. She immediately disappeared and they arrested one another. But fortunately, before they could fling themselves into the dungeons the fairy reappeared at the other end of the room.

They made another dash at her. She flew under their feet and they all landed in a heap.

'Stop all this!' commanded the King, who hadn't spoken for so long he could hardly remember how to do it. 'Silence everyone and everyone stand still. Let this young lady,' he pointed to the fairy, 'explain matters if she can.'

'Thank you, Your Majesty,' said the fairy, giving the King a fetching smile that tilted his crown over one eye. 'I shall now make one more endeavour to find the Queen's diamonds. I didn't steal them, but I think I know what happened to them.'

'Bring them back!' cried the Queen in an anguished voice,

which is an uncomfortable thing to cry in. 'Bring them back and all is forgiven.'

'If I bring them back can I stay on as Court Fairy?' asked the fairy.

'Yes, yes, anything, only bring back my diamonds,' shrieked the Queen.

'Right,' said the fairy. She hitched up her dress, stretched out her arms, waved her wand and said another spell.

There was a humming sound. Another bit of smoke landed on the table, twirled round and turned into a pork pie.

'Pah!' snorted the Queen, louder than ever. 'I knew it. She's done it again. She can't or else she won't get my diamonds back. Arrest her!'

But the guards were a bit slow in obeying the order this time, knowing what a slippery type the fairy was.

'Bring me a nice sharp knife,' said the fairy.

'Don't let her stab me!' shrieked the Queen, shrinking back against a cabinet which fell over with a royal crash.

'Tut, tut,' said the King. 'Someone fetch a knife from the kitchen and let's see what's going to happen.'

A knife was brought. The fairy took it and approached the pork pie as if she were going to cut a wedding cake.

'Behold!' she cried dramatically. And she cut the pork pie open.

Wow! And other exclamatory noises. There was the Queen's missing diamond necklace, snugly tucked inside the pie with the pork.

'You hid the necklace yourself, Your Majesty,' said the fairy. 'You did it to test my magic. I hope you're satisfied now.'

'Nonsense,' said the Queen, 'as if I'd hide my necklace in

a pork pie. I don't want to go around smelling like a super-market.'

'Oh, you didn't hide it in a pork pie,' said the fairy, 'but that was the only way I could bring it back, as I can't always be sure of what magic I'm going to do, but I'm a daisy at pork pies.' She cut a large slice and began eating it.

'I never knew fairies ate pork pies,' whispered Princess Sonia.

'Well, now you know what happened to Mum's diamonds,' said Princess Rosy, 'so you ought to be satisfied.' And they both went off to find the two Princes, while the Court Jeweller cleaned the smell of pork pie off the Queen's neck-lace and the royal palace of Incrediblania turned its attention once more to serious affairs of state such as banquets, garden parties and bazaar openings.

12

The Great Incrediblanian Election

It was breakfast time again in the royal palace of Incrediblania and, half way through his second egg, the King announced:

'I've had an idea.'

'Oh no, not again!' cried the Queen, spreading honey on her bread and wondering why it made her think of blackbirds and people hanging out clothes. 'The last time you had an idea at the breakfast table it landed my necklace in a pork pie. If you have any more, you'll probably land the kingdom in the soup.'

'Oh, very droll,' said the King, starting on the marmalade, 'but this is different. It's a more important idea. I think we should have a Parliament.'

'You're eating too much marmalade,' said the Queen. 'That's the third time the pot's been empty this week.'

'To blazes with marmalade!' said the King, taking another spoonful before it obeyed his royal command and went there. 'I think we should have an election and let the people choose a set of people to form a Parliament and help govern the country. Very democratic. Lots of other countries do it.'

'I thought we had ministers to do the governing,' said the Queen, 'though I must admit I'm always having to tell them how to do it.'

'Yes, of course,' said the King, 'but my idea is to have a Parliament full of MP sort of people who can argue and shout at one another and wave papers and throw things about in the interests of the country, while I and the ministers do the governing—with your invaluable help, of course, my dear,' he added hurriedly, as he saw the Queen getting one of her looks ready. 'It will keep the people happy thinking they're having a hand in running the country and Parliament can deal with complaints about the trains being late, or the weather a bit wet, or there being a shortage of semolina pudding, or a mountain of mince pies, or any of the other economic disasters that are always happening if there's nobody to stop them.'

'Yes, I think that's a good idea,' said the Queen, 'and I shall open the first Parliament, in a new dress, of course, and plenty of new jewels. We can't have Incrediblania doing things on the cheap.'

'The only thing is,' said the King, 'where can Parliament sit?'

'On benches,' said the Queen, 'as they do in England, where they have front benches and back benches and park benches and carpenters' benches and benches for magistrates to sit on. Everybody sits on benches in England, so it won't hurt a few MP people to sit on them here.'

'We'll have to get the carpenters busy making the benches,' said the King, 'but what I meant was, where, in what room, hall, chamber, mansion, salon, attic, basement, parlour or other enclosed space can they meet to do their parliamenting? Not in the throne-room, of course, nor the dining-room, because of parties other than parliamentary ones.'

'Why not build a House of Parliament for them,' said the Queen. 'It will make no end of employment and keep the MPs out of my way.'

'Good idea,' said the King. 'I'll have it started at once.'

'And don't put it too near the palace or close to my rose garden,' said the Queen. 'I want a bit of peace.'

'We'll put it on that field where we used to have the dragon races,' said the King, and he went off to tell plenty of people to tell no end of other people to instruct several other people to order hundreds of people to get busy building the House of Parliament.

When he'd done that, he instructed plenty more people to arrange to get other people chosen to be Members of Parliament, by fixing up polling booths where people could vote and voting forms they could put crosses on and by making arrangements for people in different parts of the kingdom to choose people to be voted for. It was going to be the busiest time in Incrediblania since the coronation, and probably the noisiest.

But behind all this highly legal and right and proper business of arranging the election to the first of all Incrediblanian Parliament, dastardly deeds were being plotted.

It was the wicked Count Bakwerdz at it again. But no, no, surely no? He was away in Nullipop washing the Nabob's pale blue elephant.

Oh, no he wasn't. Not the crafty Count Bakwerdz. But how had he managed to escape? Nullipop was a long way from Incrediblania. Surely he hadn't stolen the precious pale blue elephant and ridden it secretly home? No, no, you can't ride pale blue elephants secretly. That was something even the wily Count Bakwerdz couldn't do. Oh no, it was much simpler than that. He just made a muck up of washing the elephant. It wasn't very difficult. In fact, it was a lot easier than doing the job properly, which needs seven different kinds of tools, including one that looks like a giant-sized bottle-opener, one that might be a fifteenth-century Flemish pike but isn't, one that would do very well as an old-fashioned carpet brush and some others that look like anything or nothing, plus a sort of football goal-post arrangement for the elephant to stand in.*

So the wicked Count got his bottle-opener mixed up with his carpet brush, stood the elephant wrong way about in the goal-post and used the Nabob's wife's most expensive perfume to wash the elephant, which not only made a jumbo-sized lovely pong, but also caused a double jumbo-sized row in the palace. And they sent the wicked Count home with a flea in his ear, as the saying goes, which he found easier to deal with than an elephant on his hands.

But oh dear! He arrived back in Incrediblania just in time to start dastardly plotting for the great election. And dastardly plottings at elections are all too liable to occur without the wicked Count doing any of his own.

'Ah, ha, ha, ha, ha!' he snarled. 'This is my great chance. I shall get myself elected as an MP and cause trouble in Parliament. In fact,' he said to himself, a nasty gleam coming into his eyes as he thought of a ferociously dastardly idea, 'I shall do better than that. I shall take over Parliament, abolish the monarchy and claim the kingdom myself, ha, ha, ha!'

The great first ever Incrediblanian election was raging full out. Would-be MPs were screaming about how good and clever they were and how Incrediblania couldn't possibly survive without them. The place was thick with political parties. There were:

The Restricted Liberalists, who believed in letting every-

---

* All of this is more or less correct, according to recorded descriptions of how to wash an elephant in Ancient China (which doesn't mean in an old earthenware wash basin).

one do as they liked, so long as they themselves approved of it.

The P.P.C.P., which stood for the Party for the Promotion of Children's Parties. This was enthusiastically supported by the children who would go to the parties and by the mums

and dads who hoped for a bit of peace while they were there.

There was also the National Health Party, which was going to make everyone clean their teeth three times a day and send round dental policemen to make sure they did it.

The Public Safety Party, which intended to make a speed limit of two miles an hour and not allow anyone to stop anywhere.

The Security of the Kingdom Party, which would make

everybody join the Army so as to be ready to defeat enemies.

The Incrediblanian National Party, which believed in letting the King and the ministers do the governing, while they did nothing in particular and got well paid for it.

And finally and most drastic of all, there was the Bakwerdz Forwardz Party, which consisted of Count Bakwerdz and nobody else. It was there to put the wicked Count in control of Parliament by getting him elected two hundred times in different parts of the country.

'This is awful!' groaned the Queen, running round shutting windows to keep out the noise. 'I can't hear myself speak.'

'You don't need to,' said the King. 'You know what you've said without hearing it.'

'This election is worse than three Cup Final days and noisier than ten battles,' she complained.

'Well, voting day is tomorrow,' said the King. 'Then it will all be over.'

'No it won't,' said the Queen. 'The noise will simply shift from the streets to the House of Parliament, but, thank goodness, I shan't be able to hear it there.'

At last voting day arrived. Everybody turned out to vote except the children. They didn't have a vote, but they had the day off because all the schools were used as voting places.

All over Incrediblania there were queues. You'd have thought they were giving out free tea with strawberries and cream.

'It all seems to be going very well,' said the King. 'This idea of mine looks like being most successful.'

Then the two Princes burst in at the door waving their hands.

'Majesty Dad! Majesty Dad!' they cried both together, as

though they were singing a duet. 'Everything is terrible. The wicked Count Bakwerdz is going to seize control of your new Parliament.'

'Nonsense,' said the King, 'how can he? This Parliament will be properly and demowhat'sitly elected by the people.'

'No, no, you don't understand,' said Prince Poppup, popping up and down. 'Count Bakwerdz has put himself up for Parliament in every single one of the places in the kingdom.'

'Yes, yes,' cried Prince Egbert, 'and he's promising the people more pocket-money, extra holidays, less work, free chocolate and five assorted puddings for school dinners.'

'He's bound to get in,' wailed Prince Poppup.

'Rubbish!' cried the King. 'He can only get elected once, and then he'll be one against the rest of Parliament. He'll be a minority group.'

'No, no, he won't!' cried Prince Egbert. 'He's put himself up for every place in the kingdom and he'll get voted in everywhere. Nobody else will have a chance with all those promises he's making. He'll be the only MP in the Parliament. He'll be able to bring in a law abolishing the monarchy . . .'

'Oh, will he!' said the Queen in one of her voices. 'We shall see about that. I have no intention of being abolished and certainly not by an MP . . . Miserable Person!' And she swept out.

What a situation! The wicked Count Bakwerdz likely to be the only MP in the new Parliament and able to pass any laws he liked. How awful.

But the King wasn't disturbed.

'He can't do it,' he said. 'People won't be taken in by his wild promises. They'll know you can't have more pocket-money and more holidays. Where's the money to come from?'

But oh dear! The people of Incrediblania weren't used to elections. They took it for granted a Member of Parliament would give them what he promised. The wicked Count was even now gloating over his success. The votes were being counted and he had got himself elected everywhere. Oh, disaster!

The election was over. The new Parliament was assembled and the King was getting ready to open it.

'Where's the Queen?' he asked.

Nobody knew.

'We can't find her, Your Majesty,' said the Lord Chamberlain. 'We've looked everywhere, but she isn't there.'

'Good gracious!' cried the King. 'She can't be as difficult to find as all that, there's plenty of her to see.'

'Perhaps she's been kidnapped by the wicked Count Bakwerdz,' suggested the Lord Chamberlain, going pale green at the very thought.

'Never,' said the King. 'It would take more than ten Count Bakwerdzes to kidnap the Queen, and even then they'd wish they hadn't done it. She's probably still making up her mind what sort of outrageous dress to wear for the opening of Parliament.'

'But you can't wait for her!' cried the Lord Chamberlain. 'Parliament awaits. You must go at once.'

'Oh, all right,' said the King, putting on his crown. 'I expect she'll be there and wanting to know what kept me.'

So off he set. Trumpets blared, people cheered, bands played, hats went up in the air, flags waved.

'You'd better prepare for a shock, Majesty Dad,' said the two Princes. 'You'll find nobody in the House of Parliament but Count Bakwerdz. He's got himself elected everywhere.'

'Oh, my goodness!' cried the King. 'Whatever can I do . . . I never thought for a moment he could manage it. I can't open Parliament with only one MP standing there ready to abolish me.'

But it was too late. They had arrived and the doors of the House of Parliament were already opening. The red carpet was down. The King took a deep breath and stepped inside to face Count Bakwerdz and his threat to abolish the monarchy.

Good gracious! What a sight met his eyes! And what a sound met his ears!

The wicked Count Bakwerdz was nowhere to be seen.

The House of Parliament was crammed with MPs. So many of them had got themselves elected that there weren't enough seats for them all. So a lot of people who'd stood for Parliament and won a seat found they had to go on standing. But as they were all standing up cheering for the King, this didn't seem to matter.

'My goodness!' gasped the King. 'So the wicked Count didn't do it after all.'

'We can't understand it,' said the Princes. 'News came in from all quarters that the Count had been elected everywhere. Nobody else stood a chance.'

'I don't understand it either,' said the King, 'but thank goodness, all the same.'

'No, thank me,' said a voice. And the Queen stepped majestically out of the second best royal coach, which she'd only agreed to ride in because the King had taken the best one.

'We thought the wicked Count had kidnapped you,' said the King.

'Kidnapped me!' said the Queen in a voice that got complete silence in the House of Parliament for the first and, almost certainly, for the last time. 'Let me tell you I have dealt with the rascally Count. I have unstuck his plot.'

'But how did you do it?' said the King. 'I heard he'd been elected MP in every place in the kingdom. People voted for him in huge numbers because of all the promises he made.'

'Aha, yes,' said the Queen, 'but in his eagerness to get votes he did something that enabled me to thwart him. In every voting place he had a large placard saying, "Vote for me, Count Bakwerdz". So I told the people counting the votes that they must obey this instruction to the letter. After they'd counted the votes they wrote up the total. Then, just as it said "Count Bakwerdz", they began to count backwards. So, for example, where the Count had 50,000 votes they counted it backwards and of course it came to only 000,05 votes. Where he had 20,000 votes it came to only 000,02, and so on. And as all his opponents had at least a hundred votes he was defeated everywhere and we've got a proper Parliament.'

At this cheers broke out, Parliament was officially opened, and the King and Queen went home to the palace.

'I do hope we shan't have trouble with all those MP people,' said the Queen. 'I mean they'll go passing laws behind our backs.'

But she needn't have worried. Because every time one lot of MPs wanted to pass a law the other MPs voted against it, just because it wasn't their idea. So no laws got passed and Parliament went on raging without doing any harm.

But what about the wicked Count Bakwerdz?

Well of course the King couldn't have him arrested because he hadn't really committed any crime.

'If getting yourself voted into Parliament is a crime,' said the King, 'then we'd better build wholesale dungeons for all that noisy crowd.'

So the Count was free to sit in his grim, grey castle and plot yet more trouble for Incrediblania.